T0123233

Family Relational Health
Songs of Praise and Bible Verses Paraphrase
-A Compendium of 52 Original Songs and Hymns,
52 Paraphrased Bible Verses and 50 Recommendations
for Enrichment of Family Relational Health

ANTHONY L. GORDON, Ph.D.

authorHOUSE

AuthorHouse™
1663 Liberty Drive
Bloomington, IN 47403
www.authorhouse.com
Phone: 833-262-8899

Published by AuthorHouse 02/08/2023

ISBN: 978-1-6655-6604-9 (sc)
ISBN: 978-1-6655-6602-5 (hc)
ISBN: 978-1-6655-6603-2 (e)

Library of Congress Control Number: 2022913589

Print information available on the last page.

All scripture passages are taken from The King James Version (KJV) of the Bible.

Dedication

FRH Songs of Praise and Bible Verses Paraphrase is joyfully dedicated to the thousands of melodious voices with whom I have been privileged to identify in various ways over the decades of ministry to families around the world.

Special mention must be made first of those with whom I worked in my early, formative musical and choral years in Wilmington and Danvers Pen St. Thomas; Mt. James in St. Andrew; West Indies College, Albion, Waltham and Heatfield in Manchester; Buff Bay and Orange Bay in Portland and Port Maria in St. Mary, Jamaica.

Dedication is also in order to those who lifted the strains as the echoes of my compositions began spreading across the five SDA Conferences of the Jamaica Union, beginning at Central Jamaica Conference, Spanish Town, the major practicing ground for my professional exploits in family relational health with early songs such as "O for that Flame of Family Fire" (Song Number **29**) and The Special Chorus: "The Hearts We're Bonding for Home" (See p. 101)

The musical ripple moved into the Bahamas, Cayman Islands, Turks and Caicos Islands and gradually in the USA, Canada, Europe, Africa and the Middle East (see Special Dedication in the Introduction (See p. 20) The momentum and interest increased as more and more new songs were sung by soloists, groups and choirs and paraphrased Bible verses were read at church services, seminars, crusades and retreats that I or other presenters conducted.

The ultimate dedication is to the world-wide family to whom many of the songs and paraphrased Bible verses have been streamed on various media platforms such as Zoom, Facebook and YouTube as part of the Family Relational Health Seminar series received in thousands of homes, churches, schools, community clubs and organizations and other institutions.

Contents

Preface

FRH Songs of Praise and Bible Verses Paraphrase is a compilation of 52 originally composed family songs and 52 paraphrased Bible verses over 50 recommendations for enrichment of Family Relational Health, and is presented as a support companion to book 1 in The Family Relational Health series *Family Relational Health – A Biblical, Psycho-social Priority.* The songs could be considered as the poetic means of addressing some of the family relational issues and challenges covered in that book. In this case, the issues and challenges are sung about and therefore complementing and strengthening what will be read in the book.

By the strictest literary device standards, the work on the Bible verses is not purely paraphrasing but is varying combinations of other devices, such as parallelism, metaphor, and similes. The result is a rendition of the selected verse, maintaining as much as possible its original form, structure, and pattern to deliver an arresting, challenging, comforting, or assuring message on family relational health.

The new reading of the verse will be a relevant and contemporary application to some of the current family issues on which focus is placed. All scripture passages are taken from the King James Version (KJV) of the Bible, unless otherwise noted.

Six major standing features or components of the Christian worship are:

1. Reading/Studying of the Holy Scriptures
2. Praying to God either as, or in a combination of adoration and praise; gratitude and thanksgiving; petition and supplication
3. Testifying of His Goodness
4. Singing of Hymns and Songs

5. Exhortation or Preaching of the Word
6. The Faithful Support of the Gospel through the 4 T's of Christian Stewardship: Treasure, Time, Talent and Body Temple

From a family relational health perspective, these six features are fully provided for in the two books, making them a fitting duo to help in enhancing general or family worship at home, church, camp meeting, and other events.

The songs are not aligned to the hymnal or songbook of any particular church; therefore, the user can feel free to do his or her own cross-referencing with the local hymnal or songbook. It could be fun to make various comparisons in terms of messages and variations of the original and the newly composed song.

As has been repeatedly expressed in *Family Relational Health - A Biblical, Psycho-social Priority*, about readership sensitivity and the non-confrontational intent of the material presented, the same goes for this one. The entire content of this book, including the songs and paraphrased Bible verses, is primarily written to and for ardent, practicing, Bible-believing Christians and anyone else who genuinely desires to become knowledgeable of the biblical teaching on family relational health.

A Non-confrontational Approach

The book is *not* written to contend with, condemn, oppose, or incite ill will of any form conceivable to any individual, group, or organization of any sex, gender-orientation, racial, religious, cultural, political, or other identity.

However, the Christian families live in the same world as all others and must grapple with all the issues and challenges of the society, among which issues and challenges are some that are diametrically and vehemently openly opposed to the biblical foundation on which their faith is anchored. Leaders of the Bible-based Christian faith would have reneged in their God-given responsibility and failed in their flock-watchmanship duty if they do not do their "spiritual SWOT analysis" with emphasis on the *threats* and identify the issues that endanger the flock. They must then teach the members how to know such threats and what they ought to teach and do in their homes, churches, schools, and institutions to ward off the impact of such advancing forces. (See God's solemn warning to His under-shepherds in Ezekiel 33:1–11 and Song Number 48).

It is against that sense of God-inspired responsibility and accountability that some of the songs name or allude to some of the publicly known and potentially controversial issues, for the purpose of sensitization and education of the faithful. The underpinning nonadversarial clarion call mirroring Paul's counsel in Ephesians 6:10–12 is this: The Family Is Under Attack, Let Us Fight Back!

The "fight-back" is anchored in the uncompromising teachings of God's family book, the Holy Bible, to fortify the minds of the members and all others who will listen.

The book further acknowledges that sometimes there could be a thin or even blurred line between presenting the unadulterated, uncompromising, biblical, prophetic truth about some societal, sensitive, and controversial issues, and at the same time respecting, protecting, and preserving the inalienable human rights of everyone. Every effort is made, under the inspiration of the indwelling Holy Spirit (to Whom the origin of the songs and the paraphrased Bible verses are attributed), to deliver the unquenchable word of Bible truth with no calculated offense to anyone and more so, in the interest of love and good, Bible-based, family relational health.

Acknowledgement

The historical development of this work would not have been fully told if due credit were not paid to my son, Delthony. Originally, there were ten family relational health songs that were listed as Appendix 1 of the first book, *Family Relational Health - A Biblical, Psycho-social Priority*. Upon his overview of the book, while we sat in his church vestry, at Beavercreek Ohio, Delthony strongly suggested that I do not include them but that I give thought to increasing the number of compositions and publishing them along with the paraphrased Bible verses (about fifteen of them at that time) under separate cover.

I did not agree with his suggestion at first since my original plan was to have them as a part of the first book. However, upon returning home to St. Jago South, St. Catherine Jamaica, where most of the writing of the two books took place, under my St. Julian mango tree *(see Family Relational Health - A Biblical, Psycho-social Priority page xiv)*, I came to realize that my son's vision was further than mine and eventually yielded to his persuasion. As for the progressive increase of the number from ten to fifty-two songs, my daughter, Delthonette, is to be credited with the influence as mentioned in section 2 under the subtitle "Why Fifty-Two Songs? - Two Objectives." (See p. 25)

In my family lab, daughter-in-law, Esther, son-in-law, Andrew, and our grandchildren, Jonathan, Nathan, and Hadassah, all chimed in as we sang many of the songs during family worship. My niece, Stacy, and her husband, Delroy, affirmed the project as they sang some of the early compositions and joined us in envisioning the completion.

Deloris, my dear wife, bore the heat of the days and the silence of the late nights and early mornings, giving up her sleep in those wee hours as she stayed the course with me. She typed most of the manuscript, helped in the research, dreamed with me, and bolstered my spirit to press to the finishing line.

All told, this project is a perfect example of the family relational health laboratory discussed in Chapter 1 of *Family Relational Health - A Biblical, Psycho-social Priority*. Family members fully played their parts in seeing it come to fruition. Thanks be to the God of Families for His inspiration to all of us.

Section 1

Family Relational Health: An Introduction

Preamble to Glossary

The term *family relational health* is the golden thread that runs from cover to cover of this book. More so, in the Preface, it is stated that this book is the support companion to book 1 in the Family Relational Health series: *Family Relational Health - A Biblical, Psycho-social Priority.*

Undoubtedly, the reader will gather an understanding of the concept, principles, and practices of family relational health as he or she reads through the sectional introductory notes, sings the songs, and reads the paraphrased Bible verses.

That expectation aside, it is still considered prudent to offer a formal introduction of this new practice—family relational health care—to provide the reader with an intelligent head start into its background and an understanding as to why it is the driving thematic force behind the songs and the paraphrased Bible verses.

To best provide that intelligent head start, we will look at the definition of the terms *family, relational,* and *health* as they appear in the Glossary and at the Introduction to the subject in the first book, *Family Relational Health: A Biblical Psycho-social Priority.* In this way, the reader will be familiar with the key concepts and principles going forward, and will be even better able to appreciate the messages of family relational health in the songs and paraphrased Bible verses. It could be further helpful to familiarize oneself with the extensive vocabulary in the Glossary as well as the FRHS Original Acronyms, Syndromes and Behavioural Conditions in the Index of *Family Relational Health – A Biblical, Psycho-social Priority.*

Glossary Definitions

Family: The original, biological, historical, and biblical basic communal unit of human society, beginning with the marriage of the male and female as husband and wife respectively, and expanding with them becoming parents as father and mother, having produced another or others of their kind: offspring child(ren) as son(s)/daughter(s).

This grouping is sociologically referred to as the *nuclear family*. The generic use of the term *family* goes beyond the biological bloodline perspective and incorporates the theological, which is also called the ecclesiastical (Matt. 12:46–50), anthropological, sociological, psychological, and analytical definitions, concepts, and perspectives based on the composition and operations of the group.

Household: The communal unit of any combination of persons sharing one house as home, ideally but not necessarily beginning as a family (as defined above), but definitely headed by one who is accorded or one who assumes leadership by virtue of his or her seniority, maturity, and experience. The household can be an expansion of the family to include relatives such as cousins, in-laws, and others, and is therefore sometimes used interchangeably with its predecessor, *family.*

Relational: *Relational* means being connected to, belonging to; having to do with; being a part of. *Merriam-Webster's Collegiate Dictionary* uses the term *kinship*, which offers additional explanation on the critical nature of the term *relational*. Kinship refers to having affiliation, tie, link, likeness, similarity. In a healthy family relationship, the parties experience the deepest possible sentiments of these descriptions.

Relational refers to a state of like-mindedness, as Paul admonished the Philippians in chapter 2:2. "Fulfill ye my joy, that ye be likeminded, having the same love, being of one accord, of one mind."

When *notifiers* are carefully observed, they give an indication of the state of the four vital signs of family relational health in the person's mind. They suggest how one person connects with, interacts with, bonds with, and supports the other person. Read about *Notifiers* in Chapter 8 – The DNRA Theory of Family Relational Health in Book 1.

Health: The overall, combined, and interrelated condition of one's physiological (referring to the state and functions of the body) and psychological (referring to the state and functions of the active, sound mind) state of existence. This is in harmony with the World Health Organization's definition of health as "a state of complete physical, mental, and social well-being and not merely the absence of disease or infirmity."

Family relational health: The quality of the intra- and interpersonal relationship that exists in the active, sound mind of an individual indicated by the strength, intensity, trend, and patterns of the four psychological vital signs of *connection* (be it firm or fragile), *rapport* (be it mutual or selfish), *bond* (be it positive or negative), and *support* (be it conditional or unconditional) that affect and influence the individual's overall existence.

The quality of those vital signs is manifested in his or her thoughts, words, perceptions, actions, and general worldview on a daily basis at home between husband and wife, father and mother, parents and child/children, and siblings and relatives, providing an index to that which could be demonstrated at school, church, workplace, and society at large.

The Introduction

(From Book 1)

Family Relational Health and a Good Christian Life

There is an inextricable link between family relational health and being a good Christian. Put frankly, one cannot be a good Christian if one is not practicing and experiencing good, healthy family relationships between oneself and those in one's sphere of influence.

> If a man says, I love God, and hateth his brother, he is a liar: for he that loveth not his brother whom he hath seen, how can he love God whom he hath not seen? And this commandment have we from him, That he who loveth God love his brother also. (1 John 4:20–21)

One cannot be a good Christian if one refuses to be a good family member. The operative word here is *refuses*. If a family member does not make the necessary efforts—if such a person does not seek to equip himself or herself with family relational skills to improve the quality of the relationship between himself or herself and the significant others in his or her life—that neglect would be considered a refusal to improve family relational health. This is more so when he or she is made aware that there is room and means for improvement to be made.

But what is a healthy relationship? Why this term *relational health*, and even more pointedly, *family relational health*? (These and other terms are explained in the Glossary after Chapter 12.) And deepening the question and concern raised already, is the suggestion that the concept of family relational health is a biblical priority! On what grounds are such positions and teachings based? Are there unequivocal scriptural support for such propositions?

Physiological Health Compared with Family Relational Health

These questions are among the large array that this book will seek to answer. In the accompanying book, *Family Relational Health: A Missing Dimension in Comprehensive Health Care* (written for the medical and related communities), the point is made that there is an imbalance between the importance that mainstream society places on physiological health—the state and functions of the body—and psychological health—the state and functions of the mind.

Equally, there is a bewildering amount of evidence that the Church, in general, does not place equal importance on quality family relational health and what some would call *straight Gospel*. One needs only to see the proliferation of radio and television religious programs with an emphasis on the preaching of the Word (prophecies, eschatology, grace, law, creationism, health, and various other doctrines) as *straight* Gospel, compared to the number of such programs that focus on biblical family life. The difference is alarming and does call for an explanation.

This fact is so glaring that in some quarters, the health message is referred to as the right arm of the Gospel. It can be understood that health, especially in the physiological sense of the word, is critical to the quality of Christian life and teaching, given that it is based on God's original plan for the overall well-being of His children from the Garden of Eden (Gen. 2:9, 16; Gen. 3:22, 24; Rev. 2:7; Rev. 22:2, 14).

However, the focus on physiological health should ideally be juxtaposed with family relational health, given that sequentially the relationship impairment in the Garden of Eden preceded the consequential deterioration of physiological health in that the broken relationships in the mind took place before the degeneration of the body actually began. It stands to reason that while the health message (essentially focusing on the body temple) could correctly be seen as the right arm of the Gospel, family relational health could be seen as the foundation of the Gospel, given the correctly understood order of their announcement. There is no competition intended here as when correctly viewed, the two main aspects of health, physiological and psychological, are complementary so that the person can experience balanced, optimum health.

Today, health-focused programs in most churches are generally more structured and organized than those for family life, even with more appeal and support from some in the top leadership. One of the big promotional crowd pullers for evangelistic campaigns or Gospel outreach programs is health fairs, with many types of medical services being offered. These services range from blood pressure checks and urine analysis to mammography, pap smears, PSA blood tests, and prostate (DRE) exams, dental, optical, nutritional among others. Sometimes a family seminar/counseling component is added, but it is not always promoted with the same degree of urgency and importance to life as the health component, and the resulting attendance and participation are just as low-keyed.

Credit must be given to the many churches that pay balanced attention to family-life programs with the other aspects of church life, including health programs. Some churches host family-life crusades, retreats, conventions, and other features that focus on different aspects of the family. Some have very strong clubs and organized groups for married couples, singles, parents, seniors, and other subcategories of family life. It seems natural that the leaders of such churches not only believe in good, Bible-based family life but are themselves experiencing healthy family relationships.

The Protoevangelium and the Marriage at Cana of Galilee: Common Message

However, in the broad picture, as implied above, there seems to be an assumption that embracing the Gospel and accepting Christ automatically make one a good family member. Worse yet, it appears that most leaders in Christianity have missed the main message of the protoevangelium announced in Genesis 3:15 and that of Christ's first miracle recorded in John 2:1–11. "This beginning of miracles did Jesus in Cana of Galilee, and manifested forth his glory; and his disciples believed on him."

In the first case, the promised coming "seed" of Genesis 3:15 was to come, heal, and restore the broken family relationship and consequently the impaired family relational health that sin had caused. "And I will put enmity between thee and the woman, and between thy seed and her seed; it shall bruise thy head, and thou shalt bruise his heel."

Secondly, Christ's presence at the marriage ceremony at Cana of Galilee was the Godhead's endorsement (2 Cor. 5:18–19) and reaffirmation of God's original family blueprint, beginning with marriage.

> And all things are of God, who hath reconciled us to himself by Jesus Christ, and hath given to us the ministry of reconciliation; To wit, that God was in Christ, reconciling the world unto himself, not imputing their trespasses unto them; and hath committed unto us the word of reconciliation.

Jesus's intervention in the marriage was as divine as it was human. It was divine because it demonstrated the miracle-working power of God to meet all human needs. It was human because He saved the wedding planners from the embarrassment of being called stingy and short-sighted in planning.

These two powerful stories carry the common message of God's vested interest in our human relationships. But it is not just relationships that are to be established and maintained in families; it is *healthy* relationships that count. Those have eternal implications, and the Bible is replete, from Genesis to Revelation, with consistent lessons on this fact.

The Bible is the supreme family book, and the principles of family relational health permeate its pages. But alas! Too many of those lessons are missed, even by some of the most zealous and professed preachers and practitioners of the Word.

Fourteen popularly quoted and well-known verses of the Word have been carefully selected and used to anchor the family relational health posture of this book. They have been paraphrased and interpreted in the context of the subject itself, and will be used in each chapter to show the critical importance of our family relationship and, more specifically, family relational health, to our eternal salvation.

Potential Spiritual Disturbance

It would not be surprising if the material contained in this book could even cause some emotional and spiritual disturbances. A good case for such a possibility is the application to family relational health of Jesus's combined, three-pronged teaching about anger management and interpersonal reconciliation and making or bringing an offering (worship) to the Lord.

> But I say unto you, That whosoever is angry with his brother without a cause shall be in danger of the judgment: and whosoever shall say to his brother, Raca, shall be in danger of the council: but whosoever shall say, Thou fool, shall be in danger of hell fire. Therefore, if thou bring thy gift to the altar, and there

rememberest that thy brother hath ought against thee;
Leave there thy gift before the altar, and go thy way;
first be reconciled to thy brother, and then come and
offer thy gift. (Matt. 5:22–24)

His three-point counsel is stark and blunt.

1. Stop where you reach with your offering (worship) upon remembering that all is not well between you and your brother (family member, church member, fellow human being, or whoever).
2. Go back and address the impaired relationship.
3. Then return and continue your offering (worship) to Me.

The implied assurance is that the Lord will wait on you when points 1 and 2 take place, because that is the only time when your offering (worship) will be acceptable to Him. The message is profound. Good human relationship is an important part of divine worship. This straightforward, unambiguous approach to working on relationships, and the implication if it is not followed, could indeed be a new dimension to understanding this very arresting parable of the Lord. Packed tightly, the message here is this: good family relational health is a prerequisite for eternal life.

The explanation above is not necessarily to be taken in the fullest, literal sense of application. That is to say, if while a person is at worship in the temple, he or she remembers that all is not well between him or her and another person, he or she should stop, leave worship, find the person with whom there is a relational challenge, make it up, and then return to continue worshipping the Lord. Not at all! At the same time, he or she should consciously and conscientiously seek out every possible opportunity to find the other person and make it right after the worship service.

In fact, while there in worship, if the Holy Spirit reminds you of the strained relationship between you and the other person, you can stop or pause in your heart (mind), accept the impressions of the Spirit, and proceed to pray for the other party. You will also make a commitment that at the earliest opportunity, (which you can make a deliberate effort to bring forward), you will address the matter with him or her.

The Communion Service and Family Relational Health

Holy Communion (also called the Passover, the Eucharist, or the Lord's Supper), as one of the sacred rites of the Christian Church, serves the following purposes, as clearly taught in the Bible:

1. A symbol of the cleansing of the soul by Jesus. This is especially so through the ordinance of humility or feet-washing (John 14:4–10).
2. A lesson of humility and servanthood - not servitude. This is the second lesson from the ordinance of humility (John 14:12–17).
3. The prophecy and promise of the Great Supper of the Lamb to be celebrated in the New Jerusalem (Matt. 26:29; Mark 14:25; Luke 22:15–19; Rev. 19:7–9; 21 and 22). The date for this Great Supper could be "Day 1: Eternity."

Undoubtedly, there are other great extrapolations and deeper insights and lessons that can be drawn from the three purposes of this sacred rite of the New Testament Church. Here is one such lesson that can be extrapolated, in the context of family relational health. The Communion Service provides a much-needed opportunity for the strengthening and stabilization of strained relationships and for the healing and restoration of impaired relational health in biological and ecclesiastical (church) families.

It is for this very reason that the Communion Service is to be announced ahead of time, thus providing the opportunity to make wrongs right with each other so that when all gather at the Lord's table, none will partake unworthily (2 Cor. 11:27–33) because he or she is knowingly harboring an unhealthy relationship with a fellow worshipper.

> Wherefore whosoever shall eat this bread, and drink this cup of the Lord, unworthily, shall be guilty of the body and blood of the Lord. But let a man examine himself, and so let him eat of that bread, and drink of that cup. For he that eateth and drinketh unworthily, eateth and drinketh damnation to himself, not discerning the Lord's body. For this cause many are weak and sickly among you, and many sleep.

May the Holy Spirit of the God of Families illuminate our minds and help us to see that the quality of our human relationships is a sound, clear indicator of the quality of our relationship with Christ and ultimately our eternal relationship with the saints of all the ages. Family relational health is a biblical priority of life in the here and now and in the hereafter.

Section 2

Fifty-Two
Family Relational Health Songs

Family Relational Health Songs

Introduction

In considering a study on the history and impact of music and singing in the family, we realize that the combination of both art forms has been integral to life from the very beginning of time. Against this fact, it is important to establish a disclaimer.

This work is not done with the intent of going into any details of musicology in order to differentiate between music and singing and the various purposes that they serve individually, or any aspect of music instrumental or choral work. The material presented herein is considered limited to the context of family relational health practices and is therefore not intended to be referred to as any academic or professional authority on any other subject.

We will therefore work with the following two simple, basic understandings:

1. Music refers to the harmonious, artful combination of sounds, instrumental or vocal, especially as such sound has a positive, pleasing, delightful, inspiring, and even therapeutic effect on the mind of the listener. When the sounds do not harmonize and produce such effects, it is considered being cacophonous.
2. Singing can be simply described as the making of music with the voice. This is so when the thoughts are expressed in words and portraying various emotions and conveying different messages to the heart of the singer, as well as healthily impacting those who are hearing the singing. In capturing this sentiment, the apostle Paul admonished the brethren at Ephesus thus: "Speaking to yourselves in psalms and hymns

and spiritual songs, singing and making melody in your heart to the Lord" (Ephesians 5:19).

As stated above, it is a very challenging task to summarize this vast field of knowledge on the history and impact of music in the life of the family at home and on the society in general. For the purpose of this book, we will state it succinctly. Among the greatest gifts of our Creator to us is the physiological speech mechanism, primarily the respiration of the lungs, the phonation of the larynx, and the articulation of the mouth. The artful combination of these three physiological attributes results in inspiring music.

There is a clear consistency with the account in the Bible of the reason for the phenomenal musical ability of Lucifer, the then leader of the angelic choir and the covering cherubim in heaven. "The workmanship of thy tabrets and of thy pipes was prepared in thee in the day that thou wast created" (Ezek. 28:13). Tabrets and pipes there are referring to the aerophonic instrumentality of the voice. Little wonder that his heart was lifted up and iniquity was found in him (verse 15–17). (This could be a succinct warning for those in the music ministry of the Church.)

The combined function of these parts of the speech mechanism is the production of rhythms and melodies that the mind uses to convey various messages of the emotions and experiences to which it is exposed. Truly, we are fearfully and wonderfully made (Psalm 139:14). This phenomenal gift is yet another evidence that the human being is God's masterpiece of Creation, and they are certainly way above the animals over which they have been given dominion (Gen. 1:26–28).

David's Inspiration Is Still Ours Today

Singing could be safely called the melody and message of the soul. No one knew that better than the shepherd-psalmist, David, as the sacred record has credited most of his literary works as a composer of songs and hymns. David seemed to have experienced the widest range of emotional beauty and complexities in life. His works portrayed from exhilaration and happiness to sorrow and depression in his personal life and that of the people of God in his day.

We can further deduce that David's work was a prophetic inspiration for generations after his, right down to our present time. "Such things were written in the Scriptures long ago to teach us. And the Scriptures give us hope and encouragement as we wait patiently for God's promise to be fulfilled" (Rom. 15:4 New Living Translation)

Song and Hymn Differentiated

A song is usually a poem of praise and adoration and a hymn is usually a poem expressing prayer and supplication, when they are put to music. Both pieces of poetic compositions are used by the composer to capture some sentiments of the mind at the moment of inspiration, a deeply felt challenge, or any other expression. Sometimes that experience could come in the form of a vision, a dream, a hope, or an aspiration.

At other times, the composition could be a social commentary on what is happening around generally or in the presence or experience of the person who is composing. All the above possible backgrounds, in one way or another, account for the origin of the fifty-two family relational health songs in this book. While we have given a brief definition of a song versus a hymn, we will not be categorizing them as such in the book, as most, if not all of them, can be sung and interpreted in either way.

The Family Is Under Attack

The propelling, military-driven conviction of Family Relational Health Services International is The Family Is Under Attack; Let

Us Fight Back! The driving passion behind its repetitious use in seminars, conventions, retreats, and other family-related events could be considered reminiscent of the state of mind of the children of Israel on their journey from bondage in Egypt to their expected freedom in Canaan.

It is said that music and singing were among the main means by which their individual, family, congregational, and national spirits were kept cheerful, buoyant, and resilient as they traversed the treacherous spans of desert and mountainous terrains. These geographic and environmental difficulties were exacerbated by the never-ending threats of their demise by the enemies they encountered along the way.

As God's modern children of Israel (Gal. 3:27–29) passing through the present wilderness of sin in this world, on our way to spiritual Canaan when Christ returns, we too will be kept by the positive impact of quality songs whose lyrics speak directly to the challenges that we meet. It is understood that we encounter many of those challenges in the sensitive, behind-closed-door issues of our family life in our homes; hence, we need to sing more of them at our evening and morning worships. We need songs that will uplift the spirit of each family member and stabilize and anchor the quality of our relationships.

These songs will also help to fortify and equip us to withstand the vicious attacks coming from high academic, religious, social, and other influential stages in the society. (See the paraphrased version of Ephesians 6:10–12 at Number 3 for a further explanation of the attack.) These songs need to be sung with the clarion call signaling that we will not retreat from God's original family ideals. This is the driving objective behind the composition of the family relational health songs.

Development of the Present Songs

Credit to Existing, Celebrated Family Songs

In presenting these new songs, it is in order to recognize and give credit to some of the celebrated family hymns and songs that are known in most Christian churches over many decades. They have been used during the occasions of family life seminars and related events conducted during regular church services, camp meetings, special family retreats, and conventions, among other events.

These songs are known to have brought, and are still bringing, hope and inspiration, as well as challenge and encouragement to the individuals, families, and congregations who sing them. Ten of the most popularly known of these songs are "Lead Them My God to Thee," "Lord Bless Our Homes," "Happy the Home When God Is There," "O Perfect Love," "Jesus Loves Me This I Know," "Love at Home," "Faith of Our Fathers," "I'm So Glad I'm a Part of the Family of God," "Getting Used to the Family of God," and "Plenty of Room in the Family."

Motivation Behind the Family Relational Health Songs

The same inspiration that motivated the paraphrasing of Bible verses so as to make an immediate application in the context of the family relational issue being addressed, also accounts for the composition of these songs. As stated immediately above, there are many songs in various available hymnals and songbooks that speak to different family issues and challenges.

However, as the dynamics of family life continue to shift and develop, and as the intensity of the challenges show up in therapy sessions for the various categories of the family, and during question-and-answer sessions at seminars, and in the general day-to-day human encounters in and outside of the homes, the limitation of the existing songs to address the issues became evident. There has been the deeply felt passionate need for compositions to address some of the modern and current issues and challenges affecting the present family life, which are not addressed in the available songs.

Special Dedication

A poignant case is Song Number 49, "We Are Thinking Home." This song was composed in September 2019 during the Family Relational Health Seminar series conducted in the Middle East (Dubai). The seminar came at the end of the six-month tour series which began across Europe and continued to Kenya, Africa.

During the many interactions with the seminar participants in Al Ain, one could not miss the expressed feelings and emotions of the immigrant workers there in the "desert kingdoms," as they grappled with the adjustments, challenges, and demands at the various workplaces.

All those challenges and demands were mixed with the nostalgia they were experiencing about their families and homes in many countries far away. In addition to the immediate face-to-face encounter with those family members in the Middle East, there were similar complaints and languishings expressed by others with whom professional online therapy sessions were ongoing in other countries.

"We Are Thinking Home" was composed one early morning, after an evening of driving several miles at 160 kilometers per hour, on what appeared as ever-lengthening stretches of highways in the torrid atmosphere between two distant, luxuriously developed cities in Dubai, the epitome of opulence in that side of the world.

Occasionally during the travel, reference was made to some of the places where some immigrants worked, the conditions under which some of them honed their skills, and the impact that the combined climatic and work experience was having on them and their families in the various countries from which they came.

In that early morning, all the information of the night before came rushing back to memory and inspiration began to flow at its best. A visiting family therapist's mind could not help but being enveloped by the gravity of the challenges, and the need to convey awareness, understanding, and empathy to the group of those who would be assembled when the next seminar was to be presented. The intent of the composition was to offer understanding, solace, encouragement, and hope to them while on their working sojourn away from home.

Although the other songs in this book were not all motivated by such compelling and constraining scenes as "We Are Thinking Home," they were composed to challenge and encourage family members to aspire to higher heights and deeper depths in quality family relationships.

Thematic Motivation for Each Song

Most of the songs are focused on different themes, such as: balancing of the body and mind in Number 28, "Oh, God of Families"; stabilization and healing of relationships in Number 17, "Healing in Christ"; the sacredness and sanctity of our sexual powers in Number 33, "Our Sacred Sexuality"; commitment to the well-being of each member of the family in Number 29, "O, for That Flame of Family Fire!"; transmission of parental values to children in Number 1, "Batons of Faith"; the importance of family bonding in the Special Chorus at the end of the songs "The Hearts We're Bonding for Home"; affirming the eternal value of family relationship in Number 35, "Relationship,

Great Story!"; reassurance of God's protection under the pandemic of COVID-19 in Number 18, "Home Health Assurance"; and reflection of the garden home in Eden and projection on its restoration when Christ returns in Number 19, "Home in the Garden."

Except for Numbers 1 and 33, whose themes have a specific program connection, that of parenting and human sexuality respectively, and would therefore be sung when such presentations are made, the other songs are general and can be sung in almost any family life event. It is recommended that the event presenter or Song Leader leads the congregation into a proper interpretation of the composition of each song, so as to help in their receiving the intended message. The Topical Index at the end of the book is prepared to further assist in thematically grouping them and thus making appropriate selections easier.

General and Specific Focus

In addition to the thematic comments above, and to further assist Song Leaders and family members with a fulsome understanding and interpretation of the songs, it is important to remember that the main focus and theme of the fifty-two songs is that of the entire Family Relational Health series, which is the promotion, presentation and restoration of quality bible-based family life. This ideal needs to be anchored in the active, sound mind of every family member as he or she sings at home, at Church or wherever else any of the songs are sung.

Each song has a unique, specific focus which portrays an aspect of the main focus or theme mentioned in the above paragraph. More and wider interpretation can be deduced from each song, more so as the Holy Spirit illuminates the earnest minds as they read and sing along. There is a commonality and repetitive thread in all of the *Unique or Specific Focus/Theme*, and again, the Song Leaders should identify these and bring them to the attention of the singers.

Unique or Specific Focus/Theme - Why Begin with The *Importance*?

Each of the fifty-two *Unique or Specific Focus/Theme* begins with **The *Importance*.** The intent is to highlight the Bible-based *purpose* and *significance* for the existence of the Christian family. The *essentiality*, *substantiveness* and *prominence* that the Bible places on the Christian family in the world, might be best captured in the combined paraphrased verses of 1 Peter 2:9 and 21:

"For the prophecy came not in old time by the will of man: but holy men of God spake as they were moved by the Holy Ghost... But ye are a chosen generation, a royal priesthood, an holy nation, a peculiar people; that ye should shew forth the praises of him who hath called you out of darkness into his marvellous light."

Paraphrased in the context of family relational health: "For the Christian family came not from the beginning by the mere attraction and love of a man and woman who then get married and produce children and live happily together; but it was the God of Families who designed the pattern of their lives and inspired it into their relational minds so that they should establish healthy homes to show the light of His love and grace to a world in darkness, thereby influencing others to join them in giving glory to Him, Who has spared them from the darkness of poor family relationship and placed them in the light of loving family togetherness in Him."

Variations and Similarities

It will be observed that there are overlapping similarities and at the same time, differences in the various expressions of Importance in the songs. Each Importance is to be read and interpreted in the context of the message of its particular song, even if it sounds similar to another one. In the end, all the fifty-two songs contribute to the culminating theme of the work, that of stabilizing quality family relational health in our homes here on earth in preparation for the new life in our new homes in the earth made new, when Jesus returns.

Original Tunes and Rhythms

To ensure that the congregation could not only identify with the message of the different songs, but that they could easily sing them and be filled with the spirit and passion of the message, the tune of a popular, well-known song was selected, around which the words of the poem was composed. All tunes used are in the public domain.

Every effort has been made to keep as close to the original rhythm of each tune. However, in the process of composing, the lyrics were not juxtaposed to the scores and instrumentally accompanied but were all done aurally. Therefore, although it will be rare, there will be instances where the rhythm in a phrase of a song will be different with or without a beat from the original tune.

These variations in rhythmic patterns might also come about as poetic license had to be resorted to in order to produce the desired result of that segment of the composition. In many instances, word contraction has been used to keep as close to the original rhythm of the tune around which the song was being composed.

The most popular word contraction is what could be considered the title word of the book: *family*. In many of the songs, the contraction "fam'ly" has been used to keep the original rhythm while keeping the poetic literary message in the composition. In such cases, "fam'ly" is sung as two syllables: "fam-ly." And where it is written out fully as "family," the "i" results in it being sung as three syllables: "fam-i-ly."

Maybe the most outstanding example of words contraction used under the poetic license is seen in the chorus of Song Number 22, "In the Streets of the City." There we see the joining of "danger" and "will be" to get "danger'll"; hence, "no danger'll be there." Expanded, it means "no danger will be there." With all the minor variations mentioned above, there will be no challenge for the singers and the instrumentalist to harmonize as singing gloriously to the Lord.

Why Fifty-Two Songs? - Two Objectives

The decision to compose fifty-two songs has been an evolving one, moving firstly from the originally contemplated ten and gradually growing to twenty-five and thought to have reached its maximum at thirty, with one song being dedicated for each day of the month. This was a valued suggestion by my daughter, Delthonette, as she cheered me along the development of the project. However, as inspiration continued to flow, two driving objectives for the songs commandeered my thoughts resulting in the extension of the composition to fifty-two.

Objective 1: Family Singing at Home - This relatively large number of family songs is intended to encourage more singing of family-related songs (alongside other regular songs) during morning and evening worship at home. The more family members hear themselves singing about the ideal qualities of family life, the more they will be challenged to order their lives accordingly. This could be considered as the psychological impact of "when I hear what I sing." This means that upon hearing the ideal thoughts and words coming from the songs which I sing, I am constrained by the Holy Spirit, who inspired the compositions in the first place, to not only believe and love them, but to practice them.

A good example of this expectation and hope is the use of Song Numbers 20, "Citadel of Peace," and 49, "We're Thinking Home," and the Special Chorus, "The Hearts We're Bonding for Home." It is hoped that family members would be encouraged and challenged to embrace and practice the endearing family sentiments contained in them. Consequently, they would learn to resist any callous and indifferent attitudes toward the preservation of healthy relationships at home.

It is in this context that James counseled in chapter 1, verses 22 to 24.

> But be ye doers of the word, and not hearers only, deceiving your own selves. For if any be a hearer of the word, and not a doer, he is like unto a man beholding his natural face in a glass: For he beholdeth himself, and goeth his way, and straightway forgetteth what manner of man he was.

> Paraphrased in the context of singing, we could get this:

> You are to be practitioners of the message of the song and not merely singers of the words, mesmerizing your own selves. Because, if you only love the lyrics and enjoy the music, then you are like a self-entertaining performer loving to be seen on stage but having no real benefit to himself or others—and he keeps doing that selfish acting until he eventually loses touch with whom he was supposed to be: a singing messenger for God.

Objective 2: 'Family Song Year' - Study Discipline. Family members could challenge themselves to do a "family song year" (similar to the Bible Year reading—the structured plan to complete reading the entire Bible in one calendar year). They would sing one song weekly, even attempting memorization, until the fifty-two are sung. They could also intensify the challenge by arranging to study one paraphrased Bible verse each week alongside the song of the week.

This proposed new study discipline would not be seen as distracting from, or replacing, the regular Bible Year reading plan but would motivate the serious student of the word to a wider dimensional method of learning more about family life. Ultimately, this method would help the participant to learn more specifically about *family relational health* as anchored in God's words, the Bible, which itself is the foundation of both sets of compositions.

Ten Basis Guidelines for
FRH Song Leaders

As has been mentioned earlier, the Song Leader plays an important role in determining the quality of singing at home and more so in the congregation at Church. Here are some reminders:

1. Know the theme or focus of the event or service.

2. Where there is not an established one, conceive one for the purpose of song selection.

3. Select some appropriate songs using the Topical Index as a guide.

4. Interpret the songs in the context of the service or event, and where necessary, be prepared to give a synopsis of that interpretation such as will help the congregation to sing with clear understanding of the appropriateness of the selected song. Given that the songs are all new, read the words before singing to/with the congregation or with your family during worship at home. In this way, they will be further assisted to getting the message in the song.

5. Study the song well enough in the event there are variations in the rhythm, tempo, or any other aspect of interpretation that will help the congregation to get the full impact and inspiration from the exercise.

6. Further on in the interpretation, the Song Leader has the privilege/opportunity to employ certain techniques to emphasize specific, intentional interpretation in order to get an impact that he or she wishes the congregation to

experience. Among such possible interpretation techniques are the following:

A. *Legato*: Slowing down or holding out the notes longer for specific words or phrases. This slowing down can serve to arrest the minds of the singers to feel the passion or fervor of that particular piece.

A good example of this technique is the use of the song "Blessed Assurance" at camp meetings, conventions, and other large gatherings. At the singing of the chorus, some Song Leaders direct the singing congregation to hold out "*This … is … my … story, this … is … my … song,* praising my S … a … v … I … o … u … r … all … the … day … long."

This can also be done in the singing of Number 18, "Home Health Assurance."

B. *Staccato*: Cutting the length of notes for specific words or phrases, thereby singing faster and somewhat disjointed and detached. This faster, brisk pace produces the effect of brevity and alertness on the mind of the singers and listeners. That technique can equally arrest their attention to any message that would otherwise be lost in the regular tempo.

C. *A tempo*: Returning to the normal speed of the song and possibly coming after any of the two previous commands or directive from the Song Leader. Varying or changing the tempo or speed can have equally changing emotions on the singers and hearers, and should be studied ahead of conducting the song, if and where such changes will be desirable.

A song that serves a good example of this is Number 17, "Healing in Christ," sung to the tune "Leaning on the Everlasting Arm," which is a vivacious, bright, and assuring rhythm. However, the message from the words of the first three lines of the third stanza is nothing to be bright and happy about.

> Sorrow, wounds and hurts,
> Feelings, dread and fear,
> Cleansing, purging, O! we need repair;
> Pride we sacrifice, Christ alone suffice.

The Song Leader would therefore lead the congregation to change tempo and sing those lines slower, hence, *legato*, for example. Then engage *a tempo* to pick up the fourth line again, "Cheerfully we'll march along," since it would be faulty interpretation to sing a cheerful, marching message in the same tempo of sadness and contrition as was done for the first three lines.

7. <u>Involvement</u>. The Song Leader, in interpreting the song before the service, can decide which phrase or stanza to invite the men and women to sing separately. The same decision can be done with various subgroups of the congregations (fathers, mothers, youth, children, seniors, etc.), depending on the structure and message in the song.

8. <u>Biblical correlation</u>. An advanced means of uplifting the song service is for the Leader to find a Bible verse that anchors certain message in the song. Mention the verse (no preaching!), show the connection of both messages, and thereby increase the inspiration of the song service. It could be even more meaningful if such selected verse could be one of those paraphrased in this very book.

9. <u>Invite selections</u>. Having established the theme of the song service, (assuming that enough of the book is in

the congregations) the Leader may invite members of the congregation to make selections of their choice. The Leader needs to be alert in the event a selection does not fit into the established theme. Try to find a way to interpret it in, and not to reject it, so as to avoid dampening the spirit of the congregational participation.

10. <u>Singing a cappella</u>. From its Italian origin, *a cappella* means in "chapel style," and applied contemporarily, it means without accompaniment. Where there is instrumental accompaniment (piano, organ, strings, drums, etc.), the Song Leader can signal the pause of the accompaniment and have the voices alone at any point. That could be for producing a certain effect, such as accentuation of the voices and deep contemplation or even introspection, which otherwise could be crowded out by the instrumentation. Much discretion needs to be exercised by the Song Leader to avoid distraction instead of concentration.

Number 1: **Batons of Faith**

(Sung to the tune "Faith of Our Fathers")

Unique or Specific Focus/Theme

*The Importance of exemplary, Bible-based parenting.
Parents are to grow up their children in
the nurture and admonition of the Lord.*

1.

Batons of faith, all Bible based,
Held out by parents, children to take;
Shaping their lives, yet evil they faced,
Growing to keep the vows they make.

Chorus

Batons of faith, all Bible based,
Passed on the truth of hope and grace.

2.

Those long ago, foundation laid,
Faithfully studied, lived, proclaimed;
God's words embraced, all sacrifice made,
Down through the centuries never fade.

3.

Batons of faith, all Bible based,
Spiritual pillars, anchors of hope;
Oh, how the parents gladly sing,
Praising the Lord, their children bring.

Number 2: **Beacons of God's Love**

(Sung to the tune "Standing on the Promises")

Unique or Specific Focus/Theme

The Importance of making Christian homes and families to be witnesses of God's Love and care. Family bond and unity is a good message of the keeping power of the Gospel of Christ

1.

From creation God appointed all our homes,
Into His spiritual house be living stones;
Let our lives the story of redemption tell,
Fam'lies can live mutually well.

Chorus

Beacon, witness,
Make my home as witness of the love of Jesus;
Beacons, witnesses,
Make our homes witnesses of the love of God.

2.

On all families Satan has made attack,
Our dominion of the earth he did hijack;
Then redemption plan he targeted to fail,
But our Savior's great love did prevail.

3.

As we live each day, let's strive for one accord,
Never holding grudges, and avoid discord;
Ordering our lives as the Spirit inspires,
Lovingly doing as He requires.

4.

In obedience to the Lord we'll shine our light,
By His grace in this dark world we'll keep them bright;
Send the message of the Gospel to the world,
God's redemption plan soon be unfurled.

Number 3: **By Faith We Look Yonder**

(Sung to the tune "Sing the Wondrous Love of Jesus")

Unique or Specific Focus/Theme

The Importance of living good Christian lives now,
In preparation for eternity. Good family life is a prerequisite for eternity.

1.

Tell about the fam'ly God gave us,
Tell about the path we've trod;
Despite sin and pain and sorrows,
Hope is anchored in our God.

Chorus

Now by faith we look yonder,
Yonder when our love will perfect be;
By faith we look yonder,
And see the city Abram saw.

2.

In the vales and plains of life here,
Challenged by uncertainties;
But we keep our eyes on Jesus,
Who'll reward in certainties.

3.

Stay the course the Lord has shown us,
Cherish each relationship,
Till at last we meet in glory;
In eternal fellowship.

4.

Encourage and strengthen each other,
Strive toward the perfect life;
Then when Christ comes, He will take us
To homes where there'll be no strife.

Number 4: **Children, God's Precious Gifts**

(Sung to the tune "Jesus Loves Me This I Know")

Unique or Specific Focus/Theme
The Importance of parents maintaining their stewardship of God's children;
Helping children to grow naturally, lovingly and enjoying God's words.

1.
Each child is God's precious gift,
Into each dear family;
From our homes we should not drift,
Helping all live happily.

Chorus
God's precious gift,
Each is His child;
God's precious gift,
He'll keep us meek and mild.

2.
In the home we love to read,
All the stories in God's word;
Our young minds love to feed,
On the good news we have heard.

3.
With our brothers, sisters, friends,
Sharing is our love and joy;
Telling God's love never ends,
Even playing with our toy.

4.
Come all children, let us bring
All our gifts and talents too;
Praises unto Christ, our King,
All He tells us we will do.

Anthony L. Gordon, Ph.D.

Number 5: **Come, Families of Earth**
©2021 Anthony L. Gordon, all rights reserved.
(Sung to the tune "How Great Thou Art")

Unique or Specific Focus/Theme
The Importance of family members individually and together
responding to God's call/invitation. Assurance of God's love and care for families

1.

Oh, for the joys of family love together,
In one household,
Where hearts beat one for all;
There harmony signals the sweet forever,
By faith they hear and answer God's great call.

Refrain

Come unto Me, you families of earth,
I am your Source, your Source of joy.
Come unto Me; experience the new birth;
With Me you'll resist Satan's ploys.

2.

We, in the maze of family life meander,
In search of oneness
Joy and peace and love;
Our Savior beckons unto us,
"Look yonder!
Now tune your hearts;
The call comes from above."

3.

Along life's path,
We tend to fear each other,
Goodwill and trust, often elusive be;
Our hearts' desire
To be sister and brother,
Will be achieved
In answer to God's plea.

4.

When the Holy Spirit brings us together,
In one accord, one family at last;
With one glad voice,
We'll shout, "We'll never sever!"
We hear His voice,
Sweeter than in the past.

Number 6: **Communicate Relationship**

(Sung to the Tune "Amazing Grace")

Unique or Specific Focus/Theme

*The Importance of healthy communication towards achieving quality family life,
and its influence on our readiness for Christ's return.*

1.

The mys-tery of life we share,
From our Creator's hands;
Relationship, the binding tie,
Bound by His love and grace.

2.

Our minds He made like His own mind,
The anchor of our beings;
Communication is the key,
Quality life to find.

3.

Alas! The mys-tery of sin,
Target: relationships;
Poor listening, assumptions too,
Understanding can't win.

4.

In our relationships we try
To communicate well;
The impairment of sin is real;
Frustrated, "Lord!" we cry.

5.

When Christ comes back, relations heal,
Then through eternity,
We'll communicate peace and love,
No sin our joys to steal.

Number 7: **Conflicts in the Heart**

(Sung to the tune "Sound the Battle Cry")

Unique or Specific Focus/Theme

The Importance of understanding and effectively managing conflicts in relationships;
Maintaing healthy, Christian family relationships
despite differences and even disagreements among themselves.

1.

In the human heart, conflicts play a part,
As we live our lives day by day;
Home or church or school,
Onward as we go,
Endless search for one accord we pray.

Chorus

Pentecostal unity and love, Lord,
Help us gain them as we live along;
One heart, one mind, let us go together,
Harmony, the heartbeat of our song.

2.

As our minds connect, differences we see,
"Conquer and divide!" - sinful thought;
But the Spirit bids turn to Calvary,
On the Cross, our vict'ry was blood bought.

3.

In our lives each day, conflicts will arise,
Lord, we'll manage them by Your grace;
Give us open hearts, speaking truth in love,
As in unity we seek Your face.

4.
When at last we reach
That blessed state of mind,
And Your prayer, Lord, is fulfilled,
We shall preach and live
As You Three-in-One,
For eternity, Lord, as You willed.

Number 8: **Daughters of Eve**

(Sung to the tune "Praise Him, Praise Him, Jesus Our Blessed Redeemer")

Unique or Specific Focus/Theme

*The Importance of understanding, working towards and affirming
the original and restorative dignity and value of womanhood.*

1.

Daughters of Eve, symbols of Christ's holy bride,
God created into His image fine;
Comely women, delicate beauty with strength,
Endowed to continue Creation's plan.
Wife and mother, sister and many others,
Complete in God's divine salvation plan.
Daughters of Eve, symbols of Christ's holy bride,
Esteemed partner into God's fam'ly plan.

2.

Daughters of Eve, symbols of Christ's holy bride,
How temptation led you into the fall;
Pain and struggles distort and damage your purpose,
Compromising standards and moral grounds.
But your loving Lord, Who from the world's foundation,
Planned your rescue, restored your dignity.
Daughters of Eve, symbols of Christ's holy bride,
Live the honor God upon you bestowed.

3.

Daughters of Eve, symbols of Christ's holy bride,
God now calls you, lift up the standards high;
Pose the poise of woman of worth and of wonder,
Ladylikeness, womanhood, class, and care.
Send the message, live it, and preach and tell it,
Gender rivals, no need in Christ, we're one;
Daughters of Eve, symbols of Christ's holy bride,
Fit for marriage upon the sea of glass.

Number 9: **Fam'ly Great Beginnings**
(Sung to the tune "Wonderful Words of Life")

Unique or Specific Focus/Theme
*The Importance of knowing and preserving family heritage and using it
towards healthy family bonding in accordance with
God's ideal for family relational health.*

1.
Tell us more of our fam'ly life,
Share with us our beginning;
From our root all upon the vine,
Give us enlightening.
Take us back to Creation,
God start fam'ly relation.

Chorus
Great beginning, enlightening
Our fam'ly started in God's hand,
Great beginning, enlightening;
Love is our fam'ly band.

2.
Take us back through the ages gone,
Tell us of our heritage;
Stories how they kept coming on,
Share our fam'ly vintage.
Share their struggles and vict'ries,
Triumph o'er sin sophistries.

3.
Help us all, Lord, to understand
Where in Your plan we now stand;
May we cherish great yesteryears,
Fam'ly stalwarts we'll cheer.
As one fam'ly go forward,
On God's words moving onward.

Number 10: **Give Us Your Spirit, Lord**

(Sung to the tune "On Christ the Solid Rock")

Unique or Specific Focus/Theme

*The Importance of the indwelling Holy Spirit in the lives of family members
in order to healthily manage the challenges of life and
keeping the family together towards the coming of the Lord.*

1.

We live our lives from day to day.
Comingling along the way;
Our faces wear cross, sometimes crown,
We meet with glee and sometimes frown.

Chorus

Give us Your Spirit, Lord, to bear
Each other's burden, pain, and fear!
Or share a smile and dry a tear.

2.

Selfishness reigns supreme within,
The woeful evidence of sin;
But deep within the human mind,
The need and feeling to be kind.

3.

All is not lost, Great God Divine,
Your grace assures us 'twill be fine;
As in life's valleys, hills, and turns,
Each human heart for better yearns.

4.

When Christ shall come, oh, glorious day!
Life's crooked paths, one straightened way;
We'll meet and greet, beam face-to-face,
With vict'ry, shout, "Amazing grace!"

<u>Chorus to fourth stanza</u>
Give us Your Spirit, Lord, to share,
Such vision, all sincerely clear,
All holy smile, no sinful tear!

Number 11: **God Heals Relationships**

(Sung to the tune "Only Trust Him")

<u>Unique or Specific Focus/Theme</u>
The Importance of family members seeking God's healing power
for the relational illnesses in the minds,
thereby helping to manage the challenges and conflicts in relationships.

1.
The health of all relationships
Is God's eternal plan.
Repair, restore, and reconcile
His grace and mercy can.

<u>Refrain</u>
Listen to Him, come unto Him,
Heed the pleas you've heard;
Let your heart be subject to Him,
Take Him at His word.

2.
The first relationship impaired,
Was in the garden home;
'Twas then that God's redemption plan
Reached for sinners who roam.

3.
For all our strained relationships,
God's healing love is free;
Single or married, young or old,
Let's look to Calvary!

4.
When finally relationships
Will whole and healthy be,
We'll sing God's praise, His love and care,
Thanks for His precious plea.

Number 12: **God's Faithful Family**
(Sung to the tune "I'm Pressing on the Upward Way")

Unique or Specific Focus/Theme
*The Importance of faithfulness in family life; Our dependence on God
to keep family members committed to Him and to each other's well-being.*

1.
The faithful fam'ly in the land,
A treasured quality to find;
Like Noah and his faithful band,
Kept by the Spirit with one mind.

Chorus
Let faithfulness our watchword be,
For all the world around to see;
God's faithful fam'ly we will be,
For all the world around to see.

2.
For Joshua and his household team,
We'll serve the Lord, no questions asked,
From Abram's house faithfulness beam,
Partnership was their happy task.

3.
Down through the ages, God preserve,
Faithful families, Him to serve;
And send the message to mankind,
All is not lost, there's good to find.

4.
Unto us now the baton pass,
For faithfulness, look to the Cross;
Next will be our returning King;
Faithful rewards for fam'lies bring.

Number 13: **God's Way, No Other Way**

©2021 Anthony L. Gordon, all rights reserved.
(Sung to the tune "My Faith Has Found a Resting Place")

<u>Unique or Specific Focus/Theme</u>
*The Importance of family members commitment to God's ideal
and never compromise by yielding to the forces arrayed against them.*

1.

Our fam'ly love is anchored firm
Upon the love of God;
With hearts and minds we will confirm,
Side by side as we trod.

<u>Chorus</u>
We are convinced this is the way,
There's nothing else to say;
We stand by God's great sacred words,
And for His grace we pray.

2.

The gates of hell are raging at
Creation's great design;
Controversy, cosmic combat,
Righteousness won't resign.

3.

Temptations, oh, they can be strong!
Some challenges are great;
Constrained by Christ's love all along,
We'll stay the course all straight!

4.

We know we are not perfect yet,
There's so much room for growth;
Our faith and works will help us get
God's ideal, we'll not loathe.

Number 14: **Growing by His Grace**
(Sung to the tune "Marching to Zion")

Unique or Specific Focus/Theme
*The Importance of family members growing together by the grace of Christ,
demonstrating all the qualities of healthy relationships.*

1.

The home's a sacred place,
Where fam'ly love abides;
There interacting face-to-face
And growing steadfast by His grace;
Interact face-to-face
And growing by His grace.

Chorus
We're growing and gaining
Insights and foresights for home,
We're gaining knowledge and skills
And growing by His grace.

2.

Into our fam'ly lab
We mix and mingle free;
And in the end, there is no drab
But fam'ly love is our decree;
In the end there's no drab,
But love is our decree.

3.

Each fam'ly member's mind,
We guard with sacred trust;
Respectful and sincerely kind,
Ensuring none is ever crushed,
Respect, sincerely kind
Ensuring none is crushed.

4.

Within each heart abide,
The best outcome for all;
We stay together side by side,
Pursue the common fam'ly call,
Together side by side,
Pursue the fam'ly call.

Number 15: **Happy Families Live Together**

(Sung to the tune "Jesus What a Friend for Sinners")

Unique or Specific Focus/Theme

*The Importance of family members cherishing their healthy relationships,
affirming and holding each other together until the Lord returns.*

1.

In our homes we share together,
As from day to day we live;
Caring each as sister, brother,
Never failing love to give.

Chorus

Happy fam'lies live together,
One for all and all for one;
Loving, caring, cheering, playing,
Holding firm 'til vict'ry's won!

2.

In our homes we pray together,
For our well-being all the time;
None's a burden, none's a bother,
Low or high, we'll take the climb.

3.

In our homes we plan together,
Merge our dreams with visions far;
Move in concert, change whenever,
Mutual respect for who we are.

4.

In our homes, we fellowship,
And strive for hearts with one accord;
Faithful work and earnest worship,
Christ shall come with His reward.

Number 16: **He Leads Our Fam'ly Team**

(Sung to the tune "He Leadeth Me, O Blessed Thought")

Unique or Specific Focus/Theme
*The Importance of family members accepting the supreme leadership of the Lord
to keep them together, and to resisting Satan's efforts to divide, defeat and conquer them.*

1.
He leads our fam'ly team always,
Each member subject to His care;
Our daily plan before Him lays,
Then begin the day without fear.

Chorus
He leads our team, our fam'ly team.
Each member subject to His care;
Our lives for Him will glory beam,
Bring others to Him without fear.

2.
Under His wings there's safe retreat,
From all darts shot at us from hell;
Satan, our fam'ly can't defeat,
Of God's great leading we will tell.

3.
He leads our fam'ly team just right,
Meets our needs by His providence;
Against sin He leads us to fight,
With vict'ry as our recompense.

4.
He leads our lives in small or large,
Our faith in Him is anchored firm,
Present and future, He's in charge,
With no condition, time, or term.

Number 17: **Healing in Christ**

(Sung to the tune "Leaning on the Everlasting Arms")

Unique or Specific Focus/Theme

The Importance of family members bonding together and living in harmony as they march by faith towards the Promised Land.

1.

In this family ship,
Hearts and hands combine,
As we strive toward our health sublime;
We to Christ belong,
In this family throng,
Cheerfully we'll sing and march along.

Chorus

Bonding, healing,
Strength'ning relationships in Christ;
Bonding, healing,
Anch'ring hearts upon His Holy words.

2.

We from day to day,
On life's path relate,
Living, loving, caring, trusting too;
Health and happiness,
Christ's connectedness,
Cheerfully we'll sing and march along.

3.

Sorrow, wounds, and hurts,
Feelings, dread, and fear,
Cleansing, purging, oh, we need repair!
Pride we sacrifice, Christ alone suffice,
Cheerfully we'll sing and march along.

4.

On toward the shore,

Canaan's land in view,

With support, rapport, love ever new;

Body, mind, let's find

Health for all mankind,

Cheerfully we'll sing and march along.

Number 18: **Home Health Assurance**
(Sung to the tune "Blessed Assurance")

Unique or Specific Focus/Theme
The Importance of family coverage under the guidance of the Lord,
seeking His divine protection against the maladies of life.

1.
Home health assurance,
Coverage for all;
Health Care Provider,
Jesus, our Lord.
Against all COVID
Fam'lies stand tall;
Our homes united,
in one accord.

Chorus
We have one story,
We have one song!
Whether there's COVID,
We're strong in the Lord.
We have one story,
We have one song!
Home health assurance,
Coverage for all.

2.
Home health assurance,
Body and mind;
Benefits all in, premiums full paid.
All forms completed,
Signed in His blood;
Spirit, His Agent,
No grants need made.

3.
Home health assurance,
Coverage for all;
Against pandemics, against all sins,
Grace as God's policy destined to win;
Hearts bond together,
Pow'r in His words.

Number 19: **Home in the Garden**

(Sung to the tune "Jesus Loves Me, This I Know")

Unique or Specific Focus/Theme
*The Importance of family members remembering the origin of
the family as God created it in the Garden;
and their commitment to maintaining the ideal despite the impact of sin.*

1.
In the Garden, God came down,
And in love, They looked around;
There in paradise, They found,
Family life, Creation's crown.

Chorus
Home in the garden,
God's fam'ly started;
Home in the garden,
God's love in hearts planted.

2.
In the garden, true love grew,
Husband, wife a happy crew;
Heav'nly fam'ly joined with earth,
Angels sang in praise and mirth.

3.
In the garden, all went well,
'Til for Satan's lie they fell;
But God's Promised Seed stood tall,
Brought salvation, grace for all.

4.
In the garden, home restored,
Fam'ly love will be outpoured;
God's eternal words shall stand,
Fam'lies live in glory land.

Number 20: **Home, Citadel of Peace**
(Sung to the tune "A Shelter in the Time of Storm")

Unique or Specific Focus/Theme
*The Importance of family members working together to
making their homes that place where they all look
forward to returning when they are away.
The preservation of peace and loving stability for all in the home.*

1.

The fam'ly bond, a stronghold true,
A citadel of peace for all;
A place secure and love pursue,
A citadel of peace for all.

Chorus
Secure bonding, anchorage of hope,
Christ in us and we live in Christ,
Making home a hav'n of rest,
A citadel of peace for all.

2.

Oh home, sweet home, where e'er it be,
A palace or a humble tent;
Our hearts unite, our love flow free,
Relation health is our intent.

3.

When out beyond those sacred walls,
With yearning hearts we look back home;
No time or distance dims the call,
From love at home we'll never roam.

4.

Our home should be like heav'n on earth,
A sanctuary safe and sound;
Great fam'ly love, 'twil all it worth,
With every member heaven bound.

Number 21: **I Will Tell of Family Love**

(Sung to the tune "I Will Sing of Jesus's Love")

Unique or Specific Focus/Theme
*The Importance of family members lives testifying of the
healthy relationships they have at home;
evidence that they cherish each other and delight in being together.*

1.

Let us tell of fam'ly love,
Tell of those whose love we know;
Thank You, Lord, Your love constrains,
Forward on in life we go.

Chorus
Fam'ly love from near or far,
Greatest gift from God above;
Make us one just as You are,
Fam'ly love for one and all.

2.

Home is where our hearts abide,
Some are near, some far away;
By Your Spirit, Lord, we stay,
Close together, side by side.

3.

Separate by land and sea;
Greatest joy when we shall meet!
Fellowship, communion sweet,
May we share, Lord; hear our plea!

4.

When at last by earth or heav'n,
Fam'ly love unendless be;
May we bask in love divine,
Perfect love from You'll be giv'n.

Number 22: **In the Streets of the City**

(Sung to the tune "When He Cometh")

Unique or Specific Focus/Theme

*The Importance of leading children to look forward to the return of the Lord
and all family members being in the New Jerusalem
where there will be total safety from all the ills of life here in this present world.*

1.

When the Lord comes for the faithful
Of earth's fam'ly members;
He will take them to the new earth,
No one sin remembers.

Chorus

In the streets of the city, boys and girls will play,
Zechariah eight, verse five: no danger 'll be there,

2.

In the sanctuary, we now bring fam'lies together,
Husbands, wives, fathers, and mothers,
Parents and their children.

3.

All God's children, of all status, will be in the city,
Those who love Him and obey Him
Will pass through the gates.

4.

Fam'ly members, married, single,
Rich, poor will be all there,
No divisions, we'll be all one,
In the earth made new.

Number 23: **Just as We Are**

(Sung to the tune "Just as I Am without One Plea")

Unique or Specific Focus/Theme

*The Importance of family members seeking God's grace and mercy
to manage their present challenge and the assurance that He,
will keep the family towards the better life when Christ returns.*

1.

Receive us now, just as we are,
Our fam'ly coming from a far;
Through mix of challenges and joys,
Often happiness sin destroys.

2.

Our fam'ly faith in Thee remains,
Amidst the struggles and the strains;
Your love has kept us still together,
And by Your grace we'll not sever.

3.

Receive us now, just as we are,
Envision heaven's gates ajar;
On earth we live, work, play, and pray!
Toward the coming, glorious day.

4.

Our fam'ly faith in Thee remains,
Proclaim Your matchless glorious fames;
We're witnesses of Your salvation,
Redemption and recreation

Number 24: **Just Be Still, I'm Your Choice**

(Sung to the tune "Master, the Tempest Is Raging")

Unique or Specific Focus/Theme
The Importance of family members maintaining their faith anchored in Christ amidst the turmoil of the world against Bible-based Quality family life.

1.

The forces of hell now march promptly,
Against God's orig'nal plan,
The goal is to destroy the fam'ly;
From Eden Satan began.
Some efforts are overt, some covert,
They come in might and main,
Policies and their laws are enacted,
We know their efforts are vain.

Chorus
Our Lord whispers in assuring voice,
"Just be still, I'm your choice;
Whether they come rushing in like flood;
I'll have them stand back and declare My blood.
They'll see that it is not their might or pow'r,
But that for you, I'm your shield and tow'r."
Our Lord whispers in assuring voice,
"Just be still, I'm your choice!"
Our Lord whispers in assuring voice,
"Just be still!"

2.

The foundation marriage is questioned,
Unisexism is hailed;
Disturbed parenting is intentioned,
Male, female they say have failed.
Keeping God's words is old-fashioned,
Seen as against progress.
For Your strength we have always petitioned,
Our God, our scorn will redress.

3.

We know, Lord, the scourge will be over,
The gates of hell won't prevail;
God's words from Creation will cover
His saints and make Satan fail.
Help us 'til then to be faithful
To Your words every day,
For Your love we will always be grateful,
Continue to love and pray.

Number 25: **Let Your Family Life Beam Brightly**

(Sung to the tune "Brightly Beams Our Father's Mercy")

<u>Unique or Specific Focus/Theme</u>
The Importance of healthy public testimony of good family life;
how such can influence and even rescue others who
are groping in the darkness of ignorance
and in need of a ray of hope that better is possible and available in Christ

1.
Let your fam'ly life beam brightly,
From the hilltop loud and clear.
Do not take God's standards lightly,
Live your lives in godly fear.

<u>Chorus</u>
Let your fam'ly life beam brightly,
Send the message far and wide;
Urgent timely, treat this warming,
Heed the surging sinful tide.

2.
Bible-based truths face extinction,
Modem versions hailed instead;
Satan's plans get adoration,
We must move God's truth to spread.

3.
Christian fam'lies, every household,
Need to bond around God's word;
Let all hearts with courage stand bold,
Testify to what you've heard.

4.
Live and testify as witness,
Struggling fam'lies look for hope;
Tell them of the Lord's faithfulness,
They need not in darkness grope.

Number 26: **Loving Fam'lies Radiate the Light**

(Sung to the tune "All Things Bright and Beautiful")

Unique or Specific Focus/Theme
*The Importance of Christian families living exemplary lives
so that their qualities can permeate their communities and give hope to others.*

1.
He taught us healthy living,
Starting with marriage strong;
Good father and good mother,
Daughter, son, brother, sister.

Chorus
Loving fam'lies radiate the light
For all around to see;
Their good life in God is a sight,
That says from sin we should flee.

2.
He gave us aunties, uncles,
Some married, some single,
Cousins and grands, in-laws and all,
He wants to heed His call.

3.
Good fam'lies down the ages,
Live by the Golden Rule;
To lovingly treat all as one,
By grace we would have won.

4.
He gave us minds to love Him
And voices that we'll tell;
The joy and bliss of fam'ly life,
Made through His sacrifice.

Number 27: **Loving, Caring, Happy Families**

(Sung to the tune "There's Singing Up in Heaven")

<u>Unique or Specific Focus/Theme</u>

*The Importance of demonstrating that family members
can live harmoniously together in Christ,
despite the existence of the challenges and trials of this life.*

1.

There is harmony in fam'lies of which some have never heard,
There are couples, parents, children with minds anchored in God's word.
There are other fam'ly members all committed to the cause,
Yes, God has so many fam'lies, living by His holy laws.

<u>Chorus</u>

Loving, caring, happy families,
These testify for sure that God's grace has not left the earth.
By His pow'r we can rise up and be symbols of His love;
Then give hope to those all around us, 'til Jesus comes again.

2.

There are families who plan and work and share all vict'ries won,
Surely there are married couples whose finances merge as one;
There are singles truly happy, some resolved, some waiting too!
Oh, the children, youth, and grandp's, bright and happy, not a few.

3.

What great family reunion when in heav'n we meet at last,
When the tri'ls of earthly living fade as mem'ries of the past;
Then the angels who have never had such vict'ries great and grand,
Will just stand in awe and wonder at our joyful fam'ly band.

<u>Chorus (Last Stanza)</u>

Happy, glorious, joyful fam'ly band,
We'll celebrate the rapturous coming of our Savior, Lord;
We all in preparation for the cataclysmic scene,
The Spirit's inspiration will, keep minds in one accord.

Number 28: **Oh, God of Families**

(Sung to the tune "Great Is Thy Faithfulness")

Unique or Specific Focus/Theme
*The Importance of family members maintaining the balance
between their physiological and psychological health,
reflecting the total healthy being that God designed us to be.*

1.
Oh, God of Families,
You gave relationships,
Body and mind in one unit You made;
We lift Your name as we echo Your praises.
All sin and self now fade,
To Your honor and fame.

Chorus
Body and mind You made,
The twain should never fade,
Harmoniously You designed them to grow;
Balanced and blended in mutual movement,
Body and mind as one is Your intent.

2.
Oh, God of Families,
Anchor Your peace within,
Give us the passion for life and for love;
Wholeness we need for relational healing,
Body and mind, You made,
Oh, the fullness combined.

3.
Body and mind You made,
Combined, a wondrous being,
Made in Your image, potential unseen;
Rescue, restore, Your great mission from above,
Throughout eternity, our subject: Your love!

4.
Oh, God of Families,
Give us *connections* strong,
To build *rapport* and communicate well;
These *vital signs* of relational wholeness,
Will bond securely firm and *support* evermore.

Number 29: **O, for That Flame of Family Fire!**
(Sung to the tune "O for That Flame of Living Fire")

Unique or Specific Focus/Theme
The Importance of family members revisiting and cherishing the original healthy principles that keep each category of the family bonded and growing together.

1.

Oh, for that flame of family fire,
Which shone so bright in homes of old;
Which made each heart with love aspire,
Content and bond in one household.

2.

Where is that love, oh Lord, which dwelt
In husbands' breasts and sealed them pure?
From wives' hearts was its fragrance smelt,
Both glow committed strong and pure.

3.

That fam'ly love for every age,
Proclaimed respect and trust always;
Brightened the parents' planning page,
And nurtured children all their ways.

4.

Is not agape working now,
That grands and singles feel its pow'r?
And uncles, aunts all lived a vow,
Made home for each a mighty tow'r.

5

Remind us, Lord, of blessed ways.
Renew our hearts, Thy love restore;
Amidst the cares of modern days,
Let fam'ly love grow more and more.

Number 30: **Our Fam'ly Anchored in God's Great Love**

(Sung to the tune "We Have an Anchor")

<u>Unique or Specific Focus/Theme</u>
*The Importance of the family members maintaining their connection
on the original foundation of the principles of God's words*

1.
Will our fam'ly bond stand the test of time,
When the force of hell strike with strength sublime?
Will our love remain committed and strong,
Still embracing right and abhorring wrong?

<u>Chorus</u>
Our fam'ly anchored in God's great love,
Brought to us when Christ came from above;
We are kept together by His power,
Living by His grace every day and hour.

2.
Not by might or pow'r or intelligence,
Not by human ideal or diligence;
Quality home life in this trying time
Comes when minds unite with love divine.

3.
Healthy fam'ly homes are still possible,
Despite Satan's trial and crucible;
Of the Gospel's pow'r, our lives can tell,
If in faith we live and in love we dwell.

4.
When at last we come to the end of time,
In exalted homes, God will bid us climb;
All our earthly trials will be worth it all,
Meeting Christ and saints, never more to fall.

Number 31: **Our Fam'ly Life Anchored**
(Sung to the tune "We Have an Anchor")

Unique or Specific Focus/Theme
The Importance of the family experiencing the counsel in Colossians 2:2
"Rooted and built up in him, and stablished in the faith,
as ye have been taught, abounding therein with thanksgiving."

1.

In our fam'ly life, we are stably kept,
By the winds of strife, we will not be swept;
With our bonded hearts, kept by God's great love
We live here on earth, with our thoughts above.

Chorus
All fam'ly members feed on God's word,
Safely secured as from sin we're purged;
Never tossed about as if without hope,
Living focused lives through the Gospel scope.

2.

God's original fam'ly blueprint plan,
He began with one man and one woman,
In God's fam'ly plan, our faith remains;
Live and preach the truth on the hills and plains.

3.

In this world of sin, men run to and fro,
Teachings here and there, grand ideas flow;
But our faith is strong, and God's words confirm,
From the path of truth, we will never turn.

4.

As we wait for Christ, our Returning King,
With one voice we shout and with glad hearts sing;
We're one family from God's first design,
From its holy principles not resign.

5.

Yes, we know for sure He is on His way.
Every eye shall see in that glorious day;
We shall steadfast hold, cheering each along,
'Til all saints join happily, the rapturous song.

Number 32: **Our Lord of Families**

(Sung to the tune "My Maker and My King")

Unique or Specific Focus/Theme
*The Importance of the family members reaffirming hope in God,
and disciplining themselves through loving obedience to the hallmarks of good family life.*

1

Our Lord of families,
We look to Thee in hope,
While living in this world of sin;
We'll not in darkness grope.
While living in this world of sin,
We'll not in darkness grope.

2

Oh, help us every day
To love Thee and obey,
Help us to keep our vows always
And walk the humble way;
Help us to keep our vows always
And walk the humble way.

3

Let fam'lies heart rejoice
In Thee, our Lord and King.
Accept our praises, Lord, and
Bless our sincere offering;
Accept our praises, Lord, and
Bless our sincere offering.

4

Give us a vision clear
What You're gone to prepare,
And keep us steadfast on the path,
So when You call we'll hear;
Your trump will sound our victory;
Eternity will be here.

Number 33: **Our Sacred Sexuality**

(Sung to the tune "Before Jehovah's Awful Throne")

Unique or Specific Focus/Theme

The Importance of young people maintaining Bible-based sexual purity commitment to the sexual relationship standard of Hebrews 13: 4. "Marriage is honourable and the bed (sexual) undefiled.

1.

From the Creator's powerful hands,
Our sexuality came blessed;
Read in His words its challenges and joys.
It can create, and it destroys.

2.

Our sexual feelings God did make,
Satan deceived with his own fake;
But by God's grace we'll keep to the mark,
And of Christ's vict'ries always talk.

3.

Come, let us bond our hearts by His will,
Conquering lust at Calv'ry's Hill;
Then in the Spirit keep the 'sacred lid,'
Until the Lord says, "Now I bid!"

4.

Oh God, to Thee, our emotions give,
Purify them and help us live;
May we from day to day improve,
Sexual purity to prove.

Number 34: **Our Youth to God We Give**

(Sung to the tune "This Is My Father's World")

Unique or Specific Focus/Theme
*The Importance of young men and women committing
the quality of their youthful lives to the service of the Lord,
thereby helping to keep them on the path of religiousness, that is, right doing!*

1.

Our youth to God we give,
His service to fulfill;
For Him alone our lives we live,
Strength comes from Calvary's Hill.
Our youth to God we give,
Our best gift Lord we bring;
And ask, dear Lord, that You forgive,
In our hearts live as our King.

2.

Our skills and talents all,
For Your cause sacrifice;
We answer now to Your great call,
Nothing but all will suffice.
Our skills and talents all,
Our utmost pleasure be;
Whether we see them big or small,
Take them, Oh Lord, we plea.

3.

Our bodies and our minds,
The total offering;
All types and versions all the kinds,
You'll take despite faltering.
Our bodies and our minds,
Our precious youthful years;
Great inspiration each now finds;
We are now Your volunteers.

Number 35: **Peace, Joy, and Love**

(Sung to the tune "And Can It Be")

Unique or Specific Focus/Theme

*The Importance of family members giving evidence that amidst, the drudgery of this life,
they can still experience the evading and elusive qualities of peace, joy,
love and happiness through their sustained connection with the Lord.*

1.

It takes just one family light to shine,
And give to the world joy and peace and hope;
We'll radiate that all's not lost,
Our vict'ry symbol is the Cross.
On it Christ died, to save mankind,
To Him we'll look and in Him we'll find

Refrain

Peace, joy and love and happiness,
The languishing of the human heart.

2.

One loving heart ignites another one,
Fulfilling the Savior's loving plan;
John seventeen, twenty-and three,
The Savior's prayer to make us free.
Redemption's plan, rescue from the fall,
We live and preach the Gospel call

Refrain

Peace, joy and love and happiness,
The yearning of the human heart.

3.

So let it be, Oh God, from Your throne,
Your children's heart in accord with Yours,
And fam'ly love to all will be
Our testimony unto Thee.
We look toward the perfect day
When with one voice we all can say,

Refrain
"Peace, joy and love and happiness
The fulfillment of the human heart."

Number 36: **Relationship, Great Story**

(Sung to the tune "I Love to Tell the Story")

Unique or Specific Focus/Theme

The Importance of family members genuinely demonstrating to the world that God's original gift of good, quality relationship is still possible today, despite the general breakdown in society.

1.

Relationship, great story!
As told the ages through;
How God began in Eden,
With those created new.
All down across the cent'ries,
His grace and love proved true;
To keep His children bonded,
Unto eternity.

Chorus

Relationship, great story!
God's binding tie for fam'lies;
To make us fit for glory,
Healed from earth's vanities.

2.

Relationship, great story!
Anchors the human race;
To raise the bar and lift us
Above the din of sin.
Our Savior's great example,
Our personal Sample;
Married, single, old, or young,
Can share the bliss, divine!

3.

Relationship, great story!
Within our minds abide;
Four *vital signs* to measure,
Relational treasure.
Connection, rapport will tell,
Bond, support are they well?
Genuine, good, and sincere
Will stand the test of time.

4.

Relationship, great story!
Chapter we write each day;
Of how we treat each other,
True sister and brother.
Relationship, great story!
We'll read eternally;
The verse by verse we write here,
Lord, help us write them well!

Number 37: **Repair, Restore God's Fam'ly Plan**
(Sung to the tune "Redeemed How I Love to Proclaim It")

Unique or Specific Focus/Theme
The Importance of family members living their lives according to God's original ideals, despite the rapidly changing value systems of the world.

1.
The fam'lies of earth are in crisis,
God's fam'ly plan men slowly move;
Alternative lifestyles their basis,
The subtlety of sin to prove.

Chorus
Repair, restore,
God's original fam'ly plan,
Repair, restore,
Let's get back to where we began.

2.
The world yearns for loving relations,
Peace treaties, initiatives made;
Evasive, elusive their portions,
Deception for truth is their trade.

3.
Oh, how we are happy in God's plan,
Husbands, wives, parents, children all;
All natural to cover our life span,
We need just to obey God's call.

4.
God's family blueprint stands always,
His words can't return to Him void;
Obedience will mark our pathways,
Grace for our success He'll provide.

Number 38: **Shout to the World That All's Not Lost**

(Sung to the tune "Joy to the World")

Unique or Specific Focus/Theme
*The Importance of each Christian family testifying through their lifestyle,
that the standards upon which God established the family are still possible to be met today.*

1.
Shout to the world that all's not lost,
That love in homes abound;
Let happy families
Take their testimonies
And tell the nations round,
That God's love still abounds,
That God's love still abounds in homes around.

2.
Shout to the world, "Marriage's not done!"
Husbands and wives have fun;
That parents and children,
Brothers and sisters,
Enjoy relationship,
Loving relationship,
Sweet, loving family relationship.

3.
Shout to the world, men and women,
Still love each other pure;
Sexes' battle rages on,
There are those who vict'ry won
And live as one in Christ,
His life blood we have priced;
Our diff'ring hearts His grace has spliced.

4.

Shout, sing, and live relationship,
Sweet fam'ly fellowship;
That one for all, and all for one,
Fulfill the Savior's plan,
That we all may be one,
That we all may be one in Him.

Number 39: **Single but Not Alone**

(Sung to the tune "More about Jesus")

Unique or Specific Focus/Theme

The Importance of affirming healthy Singlehood and helping those family members to live wholesome lives, fully integrated in the bond of family fellowship.

1.

Single but with Christ, not alone,
For me His precious blood atone;
Steadfast in Him my life is hid,
Patiently doing as He bid.

Chorus

Single, but not alone!
Jesus my Lord is with me still;
Answering prayers from His throne,
Constrains my heart to do His will.

2.

Though at Creation 'twas His plan,
Two together more than one;
But since the fall by grace we can,
Live happ'ly till the vict'ry's won.

3.

Whether once married or never did,
Adjust to reality, His call;
His power will keep you from the skid,
Stay on the path and do not fall.

4.

Live sweet and sincere with all around,
Share in the beauty, love withal;
Stay with God's children, heaven bound,
Redemption's plan for one and all.

Number 40: **Stand Up, You Men of God**

(Sung to the tune "Stand Up, Stand Up for Jesus")

Unique or Specific Focus/Theme
The Importance of the men in the Christian family
maintaining their various God-appointed roles,
despite the general failure and shifting male identity in society today.

1.

This age of sin distortion and unisexism,
The men of God need stand up, speak creationism;
Male marginalization needs baptism in Christ,
We'll quit like men and be strong,
In answer to God's call.

2.

The tide of evil forces, some men renege their roles,
The missing, absent father,
World scourge of families;
Aggressive, overbearing and coarse and dominant;
Unchrist-like traits of evil to fam'lies is a loss.

3.

Now men of Christ will stand up,
Be counted as redeemed;
Come forth and stand in front line;
Answer God's call, "Send me!"
Then forth into the battle, defend God's fam'ly plan;
Courageous, bold, and valiant against the force of sin.

4.

Oh, men of all the ages. All color cline or call;
Captain Jesus is calling you unto heights sublime;
Get fitted in Christ's armor, the best that you can be,
Will help make fam'lies stable unto eternity.

Anthony L. Gordon, Ph.D.

Number 41: **Stay Side by Side**

(Sung to the tune "Abide with Me")

Unique or Specific Focus/Theme

The Importance of the Christian family publicly demonstrating the unity of its members, thereby defying the forces that are bent on destroying God's original family ideal of bond and togetherness.

1.

Stay side by side, amid the roaming tide,
Earth's troubles billow, threat'ning o'er our homes;
Some fam'lies tossed about as without hope,
But we can hold together side by side.

2.

Love's growing cold, as many tales are told,
Relationships once good are broken down;
Left by ourselves, we all would victims be,
But success side by side His grace provides.

3.

The hosts against good fam'ly life astride,
From earth's four corners they array themselves;
Discouragements, difficulties not few,
But they we'll overcome and not divide.

4.

We'll live by His grace every day and hour,
Strength'ning connection, rapport, bond, support;
These vital signs keep us anchored by faith,
So we'll together meet Christ side by side.

Number 42: **Take Our Fam'ly Life**

(Sung to the tune "Take My Life and Let It Be")

Unique or Specific Focus/Theme

*The Importance of unreserved commitment of each family
member to the ideals of God's expectations,
so that their entire being will exalt and uphold the
righteousness of relationship through Christ,
thereby leading others to Him.*

1.

We give our fam'ly life to Thee,
All in glory to Thy name;
Take our all this is our plea,
Nothing for ourselves we claim,
Nothing for ourselves we claim.

2.

All we have come from Thee, Oh Lord,
Body, sound, and active mind;
Life without Thee is cold and hard.
Loss and failure, all we find;
Loss and failure, all we find.

3.

Fam'ly members dedicate,
Married, single, aged, and young;
Vibrant, strong, or delicate,
Hail Your name with sacred tongue,
Hail Your name with sacred tongue.

4.

Every day our tributes bring,
Temple, time, talents treasures all;
Praise and thanks with joy we sing,
Hallelujah to our King;
Hallelujah to our King.

5.

All we are and have are Thine,
And surrender to Your will;
'Til Your image through us shine.
And Your mission we fulfill;
And Your mission we fulfill.

Number 43: **Tell of God's Love**

(Sung to the tune "Wonderful Power in the Blood")

Unique or Specific Focus/Theme

*The Importance of family members being heralds of God's love
in every corner of the society where their lives can penetrate through the
heaving darkness of despair and uncertainty of what constitutes good family life.*

1.

Tell of the beauty in God's fam'ly love,
Let's spread it all around,
The fam'ly Gospel sound;
Share it with nations near and far away,
The original's the only way.

Chorus

Spread around, round,
Spread the Gospel sound
Of fam'ly love, God's fam'ly love.
Spread around, round,
Spread the Gospel sound;
God's fam'ly plan is still the best.

2.

Versions will come superfluously bold,
Satanic darts abound, against the Gospel sound;
Marriage, parenting foundation is laid,
Jesus precious blood the price has paid.

3.

Hope for all fam'lies still comes from above,
Let's spread the news around,
Mercy and grace abound.
All is not lost, there's redemption's great plan
Made ready before the world began.

Number 44: The Family Altar Now We Build

(Sung to the tune "Sweet Hour of Prayer")

Unique or Specific Focus/Theme

The Importance of keeping the flames of the family altar burning bright; avoiding the dampening effects on the worth and value of family love in a society where relational coldness is destroying family life.

1.

With praise for God our hearts are filled,
As to His name this altar build;
The flames in songs are crackling loud;
We'll read His words, they make us proud.
With joyful hearts we gather here,
As all God's faithful did of old;
Like Israel when they gathered there,
We gather confident and bold.

2.

With contrite hearts, our sins confess,
And ask the Lord our lives to bless;
Around this altar we affirm,
His love and kindness all confirm.
This sacred time to God belongs,
We herald it in penitence;
Our hymns of praise and joyful songs,
We shout aloud, with no pretense.

3.

Here at this altar we address,
If there are hurts that need redress;
We demonstrate our love and care,
And shed, if must, that heartfelt tear.
Our worship time, morning or night,
Refuels us, rebonds our hearts;
Strengthen us now, with future bright,
Until Christ comes, we'll never part.

Number 45: **The Family Foundation**
(Sung to the tune "The Church Has One Foundation")

Unique or Specific Focus/Theme
*The Importance of family members anchoring their lives
and relationships on God's original ideals,
amidst the shifting and changing versions of family life in a liberal and fluid society.*

1.

Designed at the Creation,
God made the fam'ly strong;
With marriage as foundation,
Children to come along.
His plan for population,
Multiply, replenish;
Make home a stable station,
Relationship cherish.

2

All down across the ages,
His plan has known no change;
The force of evil makes rage,
Against the sacred page.
But faithful husbands and wives,
Fathers and mothers too,
All fam'ly members live lives,
God's ideal to pursue.

3.

Despite our nature fallen,
Contrary to God's will,
Morality now worsen,
While Satan exults still.
God has His faithful witness,
Who in their hearts abide,
His perfect planned completeness
Male, female side by side.

4.

Societal gender battle
Attempts another blow;
Philosophical prattle,
Would stop families grow.
But Christ said in Him we're one,
None without other be;
And vict'ry will be all won,
As every eye shall see.

5.

Then in the morrow glorious,
The pair original;
The fam'ly now victorious,
Bible foundational.
Will in eternal sunshine,
Bask bold with confidence;
As God's Creation design,
Stands as His providence.

Number 46: **This Is Our Home Sweet Home**

(Sung to the tune "Crown Him with Many Crowns")

Unique or Specific Focus/Theme
*The Importance of each family member contributing,
developing, and maintaining the cherished Christian values of a healthy home-life,
doing everything in his or her power to help each other to
be the best he or she can be through Christ.*

1.

This is our home, sweet home,
Where as loved ones we meet;
The place from which we never roam,
Where in God, we stay sweet.
We face our differences,
Affirm equality.
Respect our delicate senses,
Guard sensitivity.

2.

We honor God always,
And by His grace each stays;
Upon the paths of righteousness,
Improve our usefulness.
We're learning day by day,
The Spirit to obey;
Our talents and our gifts improve,
And indolence reprove.

3.

From home, church unto school,
We'll keep the Golden Rule;
We do for one as unto all,
And live the Gospel call.
For us Christ soon appear,
To go where He prepare;
Lord, give us now the steadfast hope,
No more in darkness grope.

Number 47: **Value Precious Memories**

(Sung to the tune "O, Come All Ye Faithful")

Unique or Specific Focus/Theme
The Importance of preserving the family identity and heritage;
Cherishing the precious memories for posterity and
healthily managing undesirable experiences
and making use of the lessons that can be gained from both.

1.

All family members, gather altogether,
Reflect on what kept us through the years around;
Cherish the mem'ries, value your beginnings.
Value the precious mem'ries,
Take nothing ere for granted;
Let's value our beginnings,
Humble or great!

2.

Our treasures of mem'ry, how we open gladly,
Anchor, stabilize, strengthen relationships;
Cheer up each other, give to God the glory.
Value the precious mem'ries,
Take nothing ere for granted;
Build future generations,
On solid past.

3.

Life's journeys, great teachers,
Nature is the textbook;
Up hills and through vales we're fellow students all.
Experience teaches, from each comes a message.
Value the precious mem'ries,
Take nothing ere for granted;
Record and stow the richness
For posterity.

4.

We move on and forward, never gazing backward.
Reflect healthily, waste no time to repine;
There's balm in Gilead for the strains and pains we bear.
Convert the failures into
Stepping-stones for tomorrow;
Review, retain, release,
Relieve, rejuvenate.

Number 48: **Watchful Fam'ly Leaders**
(Sung to the tune "Watchmen on the Walls of Zion")

Unique or Specific Focus/Theme
The Importance of family members and leaders maintaining
vigilance against the invasion of the subtle forces of evil,
and seeking to protect and preserve the ideal quality of life through Christ.

1.

Fam'ly leaders in the Lord's Church,
Can't you see the tell-tale signs?
Husbands, fathers, wives, and mothers,
Don't you read between the lines?
Brothers, sisters, look! Behold the gates of hell,
Now parade against God's structured fam'ly plan.

2.

Sound the warning, keep not silent,
Fam'ly life's under attack!
Let us rally and with one voice
Come together and fight back!
Christ says, "Be of good cheer ye shall overcome!"
And good lives we'll live through Christ who strengthens us.

3.

Let us stabilize and anchor
Our faith in God's own plan,
Raise the bar and lift the standard,
Share the truth how we began.
No evolution, but Bible Creation;
No modification, but God's redemption.

4.
All God's children, we are vanguards
Of the family ideals,
Live and tell and share the message,
Know what prophecy reveals.
Gates of hell will rise but they cannot prevail;
Christ is coming, faithful families to save.

Anthony L. Gordon, Ph.D.

Number 49: **We Are Thinking Home**
(Sung to the tune "We Are Homeward Bound")

Unique or Specific Focus/Theme
*The Importance of family members keeping connected with
their relationship when they are for-away,
cherishing the bond and doing all within their power for healthy reunion and fellowship.*

1.

Out in the desert we strive for the best,
We are thinking home, thinking home;
Working the odds like a valiant test,
We are thinking home, thinking home.
Loved ones away, in our hearts they abide,
Counting the days, all to meet side by side;
Grateful to God for His keeping and care,
We are thinking home, thinking home!

2.

Into this land with its plenteous dreams,
We are thinking home, thinking home;
Prospects and hopes, not without stress and strain,
We are thinking home, thinking home.
Climate and culture, diversities more,
Challenges great mixed with visions galore;
Grateful to God for His keeping and care,
We are thinking home, thinking home.

3.

Life way from home can become parched and dry,
Then we think of home, think of home;
Loved ones to meet, greet, and lavish with treat,
Now we yearn for home, yearn for home.
Sacrifice made in the quest for the best,
Rigors unfold north to south, east and west;
Grateful to God for His keeping and care,
We'll be going home, going home!

Number 50: **We Come, Dear Lord**

(Sung to the tune "Just as I Am")

Unique or Specific Focus/Theme

*The Importance of family members constantly recommitting their lives
to the keeping power of the Lord, seeking divine strength to witness for Him
and making it to the Kingdom when Christ returns.*

1

We come, Dear Lord with confidence,
Our faith is bold, without pretence;
Life's race we enter, Thee our Coach,
Move on to glory, no reproach.

2

We come, Dear Lord with resilience,
Revelation fourteen Saints Patience;
Our hearts are fixed, our minds are stayed,
Of nought from Satan we're afraid.

3

We come, Dear Lord, with no indifference,
For Your words our lives live in defence;
Then by Thy grace, we keep Thy laws,
And form characters without flaws.

4

We come, Dear Lord, as pure evidence,
You find in our hearts residence;
From there You beam to all the world,
Your infinite love, grace unfurled.

Number 51: **We're Looking toward Home**

(Sung to the tune "In a Little While We're Going Home")

Unique or Specific Focus/Theme

The Importance of family members placing esteemed value on home as the place to be regardless of how good and welcoming the other gatherings maybe. Once away from home, however short the time maybe, family reunion is a cherished experience and a foretaste of the grand reunion when Christ returns.

1.

When at work or school, Church
Or anywhere we go,
We look forward to returning home;
Good colleagues, classmates, and
relationships we know,
But we look toward returning home.

Chorus

We're looking toward home,
From where we never roam;
Here our faithful loved ones meet.
There we are secure in our fellowship so sweet,
Culminating all at Jesus's feet.

2.

Here is where each member's loving heart belongs,
Sacred center where God reigns supreme;
There we lift our voice in our hymns and sacred songs,
Fam'ly well-being is for all our dream.

3.

How we cherish here reunions, great or small,
We affirm and strengthen everyone!
Here we work and pray, play and enjoy one and all,
Guarding well so Satan's never won.

4.
When the great fam'ly reunion comes at last.
Where the saints of every age will be,
There we all will be, Those in Christ remained steadfast,
Since by grace from sin we'll all be free.

Number 52: **Where We Are We Will Tell**

(Sung to the tune "To God Be the Glory")

Unique or Specific Focus/Theme

*The Importance of family witnessing however, whenever,
wherever the opportunity is present and to whomsoever,
showing that a healthy, happy family life can be like a spring in the desert of this world.*

1.

All praises and glory to Christ our King,
For all in our fam'ly, our tributes we bring;
We promise by His grace to honor and tell,
Of His great providence by which we are well.

Chorus

On the plain, in the dell,
Where we are we will tell,
Of His love, of His care, of His grace to us all,
We'll tell His glory to all who will hear,
Encourage earth's fam'lies to heed God's great call.

2.

How perfect and good to submit to His will,
In loving obedience, we learn to be still;
With simple assurance and confidence bold,
We order our lives as good fam'lies of old.

3.

Wonderful assurance contained in His word,
Such blessing for those who believe what they've heard;
Our eyes have not seen, nor have entered our mind,
The treasures of glory, the faithful will find.

Special Chorus: **The Hearts We're Bonding For Home**
(Sung to the tune of the Chorus "We're Together Again")

NB: A chorus is a number of lines sung after each stanza in a song.

This composition is considered "special" for two reasons.

1. It was composed as the theme song (chorus) for the many family life seminars/crusades conducted between 1997 and 2014.
2. It is not like the fifty-two songs with two or more stanzas, with or without a chorus or refrain.

1.
The hearts we're bonding for home,
To make them God's throne,
So that out of them flow
Good deeds to show;
Husband, wife and father, mother,
Sisters and brothers,
Uncles, aunts in the band,
With cousins and grands.

2.
We'll live as one for all,
And all live for one,
United we'll stand,
Divided we'll fall;
Hands and hearts into the Lord's hand,
Such secure fam'ly bond,
Where together we'll grow,
His will to know.

(Repeat first stanza.)
The hearts we're bonding for home,
To make them God's throne,
So that out of them flow
Good deeds to show;
Husband, wife and father, mother,
Sisters and brothers,
Uncles, aunts in the band,
With cousins and grands.

Special Poem
Oh, for an Earnest Listening Ear!

Introduction

One of the greatest relational skills needed to foster healthy relationships is simply good listening. There is probably no greater sense of value and self-esteem than to know that one is being heard and, better still, is being listened to. The fact is, we can hear what the other person is saying, even when we are not necessarily listening. We hear with our ears, but we listen with our minds—the relational minds.

Healthy family relational listening is a key indicator as to the quality of the relationship between husbands and wives, parents and children, and the other combinations of family members. The same principle of active, un-preemptive, nonprejudicial, objective listening is necessary in all other types of relationships, because each person needs the assurance that what he or she has to say was valued enough by the other one, so as to be listened to.

The message and sentiment of this poem is the yearning of the relational mind for an active, listening ear. The "ear" is the visible representative of the other person's active, sound mind, with which the first one is seeking to connect and interact. That is why sometimes we hear the passionate appeal: "Lend me a listening ear! The poem was not composed nebulously or from the mere exercise of poetic and literary skills, capturing the feelings and impressions of people in general.

Instead, it was composed in *real time*, in *personal time* and *personal* experience! It captures the very live, intense yearning of the mind as the author sat alone and lonely that day at the root of that cluster of bamboo trees, near that very lush, green, and well-manicured golf course.

This, after meandering from his office, with the strain of business weighing heavily on his mind, with no one at the time to share it but himself. The pencil in his hand found company with a piece of paper that he saw nearby, and both provided him an outlet for the expressions of the depth of his soul as expressed in the Poem.

Oh, for an Earnest Listening Ear!

1.

In these days of stress and strain,
We're caught in the clutches of the rival game.
Amidst the roar, we'll wend in pain,
To reach, to grasp for survival and fame.
Oh, for an earnest listening ear,
In this deafening tumult of strife and care.

2.

"Thy man for thyself," they say.
It's the fittest, you see, who survives the race.
They shout, "Forward to the fray!"
Who will hear or care for those of lesser pace?
Oh, for an earnest, listening ear,
On this frightening path,
Stained with hidden tears.

3.

Oh, for an earnest, listening ear,
Tuned with love and confidentiality;
Who will stop, a friend to cheer,
While talking of life and its reality?
Oh, for an earnest listening ear,
That will brighten the way with
comfort and cheer.

Listening Ear Application Exercise

Introduction:

The following Exercises are intended primarily for situations of a family relational health matter, and are not offered to relate generally with matters of religious, theological, political or mere social or friendly listening.

After reading the Special Poem, it might be a good idea to do some introspective work:

1. Do I recall ever wishing or feeling the need for someone to simply Listen to me?

2. When I need someone to listen to me, do I necessarily want suggestions or answers or just to be heard ... at least first, before any input is offered?

3. Can I recall ever having experienced Numbers 1 and 2 above? How did it make me feel?

4. Have I ever offered or worse yet, *denied* anyone's request for my Listening Ear? If so, why did I?

5. Remember the following good qualities of an active, sound healthy listening ear/mind:

    (a) Listen without Pre-emption or that feeling that "I already know what he/she is going to say!"

    (b) Listen without Prejudice: Keep your mind objective and open

(c) Listen Actively - Give the person evidence that you are really *listening* and not merely *hearing*.

(d) Do not listen Patronizingly, by coldly responding: "Well at least you can't say I did not listen to you!" Be kind, show genuine interest, even if you do not have answers or suggestions to give.

(e) Choosing to Listen - If for any reason you are aware of what the person might be interested to share with you, and you are convinced (healthily, that is for a good reason) that you are not able to offer that *Listening Ear*, be kind and sensitive in telling him or her that you are not able, or that you do not think it is a good idea in his or her or your both interest for you to hear about the matter.

In a case like this, do not merely shrug him or her off. Be calm, be sincere, speak slowly and simply. State your position. If possible, and you can genuinely suggest anyone who you believe might be a better, even more appropriate *Listening Ear*, (such as a professional/clinical therapist) consider making that suggestion. If not, or even along with that suggestion, be sincere and genuine in offering/promising to help him or her by praying to the Lord on his/her behalf.

Section 3

Fifty-Two
Paraphrased Bible Verses
For Family Relational Health

FRH Paraphrased Bible Verses

Introduction

Why paraphrase? (Please read again what is written in the Preface about *literary devices*, of which paraphrasing is one p. ix .)

The writing technique of *paraphrasing* is employed in this book to achieve an immediately, direct, applicable use of a quotation in the context of the case or issue under discussion. The Bible verses are paraphrased for that expressed purpose.

Throughout the work of family relational health, the Bible is repeatedly referred to as "God's Family Book," but not every text in the Bible seems to speak directly and immediately to a specific family issue. Paraphrasing of selected Bible verses is done to achieve that goal of immediate application to the particular family relational issue being addressed.

Of the fifty-two paraphrased verses from the Old Testament and the New Testament, fourteen are used as Anchor Texts in the twelve chapters of the first book in the Family Relational Health series, *Family Relational Health - A Biblical, Psycho-social Priority*. Those Anchor Texts are presented in the first fifteen of the fifty-two paraphrases below and in the chronological order of the chapters of the book.

What is an Anchor Text? The concept of an *anchor* is employed from the sailing ship that comes to dock in the harbor. The water in the harbor is very deep, and there are times when the waves might be heavy and could cause the ship to be less than steady as is desirable for the unloading or loading of cargo or other activities. To avoid the ship from drifting, tossing, and rocking unduly, the captain is said to "drop the anchor" so as to keep the ship steady in the port.

The *Seminar Anchor Text* is that Bible verse around which the entire book, chapter or seminar is built, or around which a sermon will be presented. Even when there are many other supporting Bible passages, that which will hold the entire presentation together and duly focused is the *Anchor Text*. Seminar participants are urged to remember the *Anchor Text*, and the Holy Spirit will bring back to their minds that which they have faithfully studied around that text (John 14:26).

Text Commentary

Following each paraphrased verse is a short commentary which is intended to offer some elucidation of the text in the context of the topic. The commentary is in some cases short and may not cover in fullest detail all that could be extrapolated from the text. The Reader is encouraged to acquire the main book, *Family Relational Health -A Biblical, Psycho-social Priority*, and by reading the entire chapter from which the commentary is taken, he or she will receive the deeper understanding of the application of the paraphrased text.

The commentaries below are in two categories: *Anchor Text Commentary*, because it is linked directly to the Anchor Text of the chapter mentioned, and *Supportive Commentary*, because it is taken from elsewhere in the book but not necessarily linked directly to the Anchor Text.

Motivation behind the Selection of the Verses

As in the case of the motivation behind the selection of the topics under which the songs were composed, it has been essentially so with the selection of the Bible verses for paraphrasing. None were arbitrarily selected but were inspired at different times, settings, and conditions.

The earliest verses to have been paraphrased (and in the order as they are listed here) were:

- Number 6, Luke 4:16–18, which is considered Jesus's mission statement, paraphrased as the Church's mission statement for families, and commented on under the topic of "Terrestrial and Cosmic Relational Toxicity"
- Number 5—Hosea 4:6, which is commented on under the topic "Rejection of Family Knowledge"
- Number 3 (and later 18), Ephesians 6:10–12, which is commented on under the topics "The Deteriorating Standards of Family Life" and "Sentenced to Hard Labor" respectively, the latter being with direct reference to men abdicating their God-given roles in the family)

The Family Relational Health Laboratory

Reflecting on the development of the family relational health laboratory as detailed in chapter 1 of *Family Relational Health - A Biblical, Psycho-social Priority,* there is the vivid memory of how my mind was passionately enveloped in the challenges and issues of the families with whom I worked in the various evolving capacities as teacher, principal, chaplain, college and conference departmental director, family counselor, communications director, and human resources director.

In these advanced and evolving capacities, the wider and more intense gamut of 'the behind-closed-door' family relational issues and challenges was met. From the single, repeated, and multiple face-to-face sessions for individuals, couples, and groups, the exposure expanded. Hundreds of active, sound relational minds, in the persons of fiancés and fiancées, husbands and wives, parents and children, siblings, grands, steps, in-laws, uncles and aunts, cousins, and all the other categories of family members, at home, church, school and the work place have been seen annually, growing into thousands over the decades. All these opened up their relational minds for treatment of the various relational illnesses that affected their relationships. To better understand the concept of family relational illnesses, see pp. 412 & 413 of *Family Relational Health a Biblical, Psycho-social Priority.*

As I sought and pursued further academic, professional, and clinical training and the development of competence grew over the years, I did so with the balanced conviction that, God's words, the Holy Bible, His manual for families, ought to be the final anchor for the treatment plan that I would devise for my clients. I maintained that conviction with due respect for clients of non-Christian or non-religious beliefs and have never imposed any religious position upon such persons.

With that conviction remaining in place alongside the professional, ethical standard of non-imposition, the Holy Spirit took over and honored that sincerity by illuminating my mind. I was able to see how Bible verses upon Bible verses could be interpreted and hence paraphrased in the context of the family issues and challenges to which I was addressing my mind in order to provide treatment for my clients.

Those three verses mentioned before set the pace, and inspiration continued to flow way beyond my understanding, even to this time of writing. As family relational issues and challenges continued to rise before me, and as I sought to find answers in my professional and clinical skills and competence, I further found certitude and anchorage in the inspiration to find appropriate Bible verses that I could further paraphrase and give spiritual/psychosocial credence to the treatment plan.

God does work in mysterious ways to advance His mission through His servants. One of the methods He uses is fellow human validation for the work that we sincerely do. Such was the case of the comments and challenge of Dr. Denton Rhone, then chair of Department of Religion and Theology of West Indies College (now Northern Caribbean University)

In fulfilling an assignment for Dr. Rhone for a religion course that I was pursuing, I wrote on the mission of the Church to families. I anchored my presentation on Luke 4:16–18 and for the first time made a public showing of my paraphrase. (See Number 6). Dr. Rhone lauded the work and affirmed my composition. He then gave me encouragement and a challenge, publicly, right there in the class. "You should consider paraphrasing the Bible in the context of family life. Take it seriously, based on what you have done here. You can do it!"

Over the next twenty-plus years, as I continuously did paraphrasing, Dr. Rhone's words, the epitome of inspiration from the Lord, remained a propelling challenge and encouragement to me. From time to time, the chief 'specimen' in my immediate family lab, my dear wife, Deloris, would remind me of how I used a Bible verse in a presentation, and sometimes suggested that I consider it for paraphrasing. The more I paraphrased, the more inspiration came through as I inclined my mind to find sound, biblical support for the professional care that I offer for the family relational issues and challenges of my clients.

Thus we moved from the first three - Numbers 3, 5, 6, then 18, and the remaining forty-eight evolved as what could be called needs-based paraphrasing. That is to say, as the seminars were developed; as new therapy needs emerged and as new relational situations arose, one of the instinctive responses would be: What Bible verse could be paraphrased and contemporised to give anchorage to this case or need. Several other Bible verses have been subsequently and continuously paraphrased with the possible view of a second publication as the Spirit will give impression and utterance.

Number 1: **Galatians 5:22–23**
But the fruit of the Spirit is love, joy, peace,
longsuffering, gentleness, goodness,
faith, meekness, temperance:
against such there is no law.

Paraphrased for Families
(Main Focus: the family in general)

(Characteristic of a maturing, relationally healthy Christian)
For the characteristic of a maturing,relationally healthy person is
genuineness, graciousness, honesty,
humility, simplicity, sincerity,
sweetness, thoughtfulness, and thoroughness;
against such and similar characteristic no one can truly judge you
as being immature, unfriendly, and unkind.

****

Anchor Text Commentary from *Family Relational Health - A Biblical, Psycho-social Priority*: Chapter 1

The Fruit of the Spirit Applied in the Family Lab

It is important to take note that in the original text, the fruit is referred to in the singular number: "the *fruit* of the Spirit *is*" and not "the *fruits* of the Spirit *are*." The message to be learned here is that a person cannot possess one aspect of the character of the Spirit and not possess the others. All the parts work in sync to make the whole fruit. So one cannot be truly loving or joyful and cantankerous and impatient with others. There is no such thing as having a part of the Spirit, as in having a slice of a fruit. A slice of the fruit is simply not the whole fruit.

When the Holy Spirit infuses the mind, that infusion permeates the entire being, and the lifestyle and behavior harmonize with the total character of the Spirit Himself. Understandably, there will be the occasional evidence of human frailty, but such evidence is to be the exception and not the rule in the lifestyle. God does understand that, having assured us in Psalm 103:13–14, "Like as a father pitieth his children, so the LORD pitieth them that fear him. For He knoweth our frame; He remembereth that we are dust, that He knows that we are flesh."

It is understood that there is room for growth, and that this requires symmetrical development of character in the *many-parts-one-fruit* or the *all-in-one, one-in-all* teaching. There is provision and room for our timely development. We all do not develop at the same rate, biologically and physically. To the same extent that our metabolism, nutritional assimilation and the resultant growth and development rates of our bodies differ, so do our personal qualities, strengths, personalities and integrities take time to result in the desirable characters that we want to admire and cherish. They do not all take place simultaneously. (*CPH²*)

Remember: The above is an extract from Chapter 1. To get a clearer, deeper, fuller understanding and application of the text and topic, read the complete chapter in *Family Relational Health – A Biblical, Psycho-social Priority.*

Number 2: **Galatians 5:22–23**
But the fruit of the Spirit is love, joy, peace,
longsuffering, gentleness, goodness,
faith, meekness, temperance:
against such there is no law.

Paraphrased for Families
(Main Focus: the family in general)

(Characteristics of a failing, relationally unhealthy Christian)
For the characteristics of a failing,
Relationally unhealthy person are
harshness, strictness, insensitivity, rigidity,
abrasiveness, mean-spiritedness, hypersensitivity,
tactlessness, and spitefulness;
with these and similar characteristics of relationship,
you should not be found.

****

Anchor Text Commentary from *Family Relational Health - A Biblical, Psycho-social Priority*: Chapter 1

The Fruit of the Spirit Applied in the Family Lab

At the same time, the *many-parts; all-in-one, one-in-all-fruit* teaching of James 2:8 discourages and abhors any attitude of mind that consciously seeks to highlight and even go on to live one quality or aspect of the character of the Spirit over the other. We should strive, by His grace to grow and develop symmetrically, demonstrating all the qualities of the fruit of the Spirit.

In the same breath, the practicing relationally unhealthy person can hardly display one feature of the undesirable characteristics without evidence or trace of the others. Harshness and spitefulness, for example, can be seen in those who are insensitive, rigid, or unkind.

Notwithstanding, there are hypocrites who are adept at showing selected characteristics and behaving the opposite at other times and places. Such persons cannot last for long without being found out. "But if ye will not do so, behold, ye have sinned against the LORD: and be sure your sin will find you out" (Num. 32:23).

Remember: The above is an extract from Chapter 1. To get a clearer, deeper, fuller understanding and application of the text and topic, read the complete chapter in *Family Relational Health – A Biblical, Psycho-social Priority*.

Number 3: **Ephesians 6:12**

For we wrestle not against flesh and blood,
but against principalities, against powers,
against the rulers of the darkness of this world,
against spiritual wickedness in high places.

Paraphrased for Families
(Main Focus: the family in general)

For we wrestle not against ordinary marital,
parental, and general family relational challenges
but against the continuous deteriorating standards of this world;
against the subtle forces set at destroying
God's original family ideals;
against the corrupt, immoral practices of this age,
operating from high academic, religious, social,
and other influential stages in the society.

****

Anchor Text Commentary from *Family Relational Health - A Biblical, Psycho-social Priority:* Chapter 2

The Deteriorating Standards Against Family Life

The devil is undoubtedly a master strategist, crafty and cunning at his art of deception and destruction. In his demolition strategy for the Church and society at large, he takes the approach of the natural disaster, earthquake, rather than that of a hurricane. A hurricane does its destructive work mainly from the top. Its primary target is the roof of the house. Invariably, even when it succeeds in decapitating the house, the walls, columns and floor remain intact, depending on the nature of the material and the quality of the construction.

On the other hand, the earthquake strikes at the foundation of the structure. Once the bedrock, the anchor or the substratum shakes, cracks and breaks up, the super-structure naturally comes crumbling down. If the family is still considered as the nucleus, the core, and the anchor of the society, then it goes without saying that the answer to destroying the society and all its superstructures lies in destroying the families that comprise that society.

Many of the deteriorating standards that affect quality, Bible-based family life today cannot be seen by the ordinary eye, simply because we are not wrestling against *ordinary* marital, parental, and other general family challenges. These challenges are *covidic* in nature. The present COVID-19 pandemic has the world in bewilderment, and one of the crying comments of just about everyone is "And you can't even see it!"

That is very characteristic of the many issues and challenges eating away at quality family life. They are simply not seen until their devastating presence is felt and their work of destruction is well underway. Families need their relational eyes to be washed with "eye salve" (Rev. 3:18) that only the spiritual lachrymal glands can produce under the inspiration of the Holy Spirit.

Remember: The above is an extract from Chapter 2. To get a clearer, deeper, fuller understanding and application of the text and topic, read the complete chapter in *Family Relational Health – A Biblical, Psycho-social Priority.*

Number 4: **3 John 2**
Beloved, I wish above all things
that thou mayest prosper and be in health,
even as thy soul prospereth.

Paraphrased for Families
(Main Focus: the family in general)

Dear members of the household or family of faith,
my greatest wish for you is that you succeed,
get ahead in life, do well, enjoy living
good, and be healthy physically,
mentally, emotionally, socially, and relationally,
to the same extent that you are prospering spirituality
in a healthy relationship with God and your
fellow church members and in your witnessing and evangelistic life.

****

Anchor Text Commentary from *Family Relational Health - A Biblical. Psycho-social Priority:* Chapter 3

As we compare Paul's wish for our prosperity in health to our soul prosperity, the poignant question is this: how does the Christian measure or give evidence that his soul is prospering or that he is prospering spiritually?

Measuring the Prospering Soul

Firstly, he measures his spirituality by the pattern of his deep, inner conviction of the living presence of God. He measures the same trend by the intensity of his prayer life and study of God's words. He measures his soul prosperity by the depth, simplicity, sweetness, sincerity, and genuineness of his relationship with those "beloved" of the household of faith, beginning with those in his own family and household.

The Christian knows if his soul is prospering by the intensity of his witnessing through his lifestyle, words, and works. He knows the level of soul prosperity based on the level of the rapport that takes place between his mind, conscience, heart, and the Holy Spirit.

When we summarize all those tests and assessments of determining the quality of our soul or spiritual prosperity, it boils down to one word: relationship. Are we prospering? Are we doing well in our relationship with God? Are we getting ahead in our relationship with those of the household or family of faith? How are we doing with our relationship in the community by living and witnessing?

Remember: The above is an extract from Chapter 3. To get a clearer, deeper, fuller understanding and application of the text and topic, read the complete chapter in *Family Relational Health – A Biblical, Psycho-social Priority.*

Number 5: **Hosea 4:6**
My people are destroyed for lack of Knowledge ...

Paraphrased for Families
(Main Focus: the family in general)

Many family relationships have been, are being, and will be destroyed due to the lack of knowledge about the vital signs of their God-given family relational health and the necessary skills to improve it.

****

Anchor Text Commentary from *Family Relational Health - A Biblical, Psycho-social Priority:* Chapter 4

Rejection of Family Knowledge

Before God made that lamenting pronouncement in Hosea 4 about the imminent destruction of His people, He had presented a litany of family relational grievous ills of which they were guilty (verses 1–5): lying, swearing, murders, adultery, and similar immoralities. Sounds like He was talking about our present, twenty-first century societal ills. Prophetically, He was!

In so many cases, the records of the Bible are as prophetic as they are historical. That is what Paul in Romans 15:4 and 1 Corinthians 10:11 was teaching. It is not enough to read about the errors, mistakes, and failures of previous generations. The records were preserved in the interest of posterity, with the hope that those who came after would not mount the same horse and gallop down the same road. But alas! We never seem to learn.

Being Lost with Light in Hand

It is pathetic that in this age of enlightenment when the prophecy that *"knowledge shall increase"* (Daniel 12:4) is being continuously fulfilled, we are witnessing the continuous decline and disintegration of quality human and family life.

The application of this section of our paraphrased verse "*many families are being destroyed for lack of knowledge*" is a perfect example of a man being lost with the light in his hand. Why is he lost? The first and obvious reason is that he never turned on the light. The second reason is a remote likelihood, but not improbable - he did not know how to turn on, or how to use the light.

The above is an extract from Chapter 4. To get a clearer, deeper, fuller understanding and application of the text and topic, read the complete chapter in *Family Relational Health – A Biblical, Psychosocial Priority.*

Number 6: **Luke 4:18–19**

The Spirit of the Lord is upon me,
because he hath anointed me to preach the gospel to the poor;
he hath sent me to heal the brokenhearted,
to preach deliverance to the captives,
and recovering of sight to the blind,
to set at liberty them that are bruise,
To preach the acceptable year of the Lord.

Paraphrased for Families
(Main Focus: the family in general)

The Spirit of the Lord is within the church
which He has appointed to preach
The Gospel of good family relationship
to the poor and wounded family members;
He has sent the church to heal the brokenhearted
spouses, parents, children, and singles;
To preach deliverance to the captives of
unholy deadlock instead of holy wedlock;
The recovery of the sight of loving admiration
for spouses and others in the family;
To set at liberty those family members who are
spiritually, emotionally, socially, and relationally oppressed;
To preach the acceptable time for family reunion
In preparation for the Lord's return.

****

Anchor Text Commentary from *Family Relational Health - A Biblical, Psycho-social Priority:* Chapter 5

Terrestrial and Cosmic Relational Toxicity

The relational environment in which families live today, inside and outside of the Church, is negatively charged with relational toxicity from a combination of terrestrial and cosmic forces. It is not in any way ordinary; therefore, it requires more than ordinary treatment, as is customary of many Church clinicians. It would fall into the category of "this kind ..." that Jesus spoke about in Matthew 17:21 and Mark 9:29.

Church leaders will therefore need to heed the counsel to "anoint thine eyes with eye salve" (Rev. 3:18) so that they can discern the true source and nature of family relational illnesses and equip themselves to treat them accordingly.

When there is an outbreak of certain diseases, the medical team has to know the environmental conditions under which they are going to work. They know that they need to be armed, equipped, and prepared. They have to get proper briefing on the existing conditions and what they will be up against. In the case of an outbreak of Ebola, for example, and more currently, that of the 2020 Covid19 Coronavirus Pandemic, responding members of the medical and support teams inclusive of *Doctors Without Borders* or *Medecins Sans Frontieres (MSF)* among other first responders, have to go through the preparation protocol before they can arrive on the scene to offer professional help. Doctors wanting to help cannot just get up and go. They have to be properly prepared with their necessary PPEs – PFP3 Masks, Visors, Goggles, Long-sleeve Gowns.

Similarly, those who treat relational illnesses in the homes, the Church and in the community must be properly prepared to offer the necessary assistance, or they, along with those they went to help, will all be victims. Mere willingness and spiritual exuberance will not be able to minister to the on-going outbreak of relational illness in the Church today.

Remember: The above is an extract from Chapter 5. To get a clearer, deeper, fuller understanding and application of the text and topic, read the complete chapter in *Family Relational Health – A Biblical, Psycho-social Priority*.

Number 7: **Hebrews 4:12**

For the word of God is quick, and powerful, and sharper than any two-edged sword, piercing even to the dividing asunder of soul and spirit, and of the joints and marrow, and is a discerner of the thoughts and intents of the heart.

Paraphrased for Families
(Main Focus: the family in general)

For the family relational counsel and guidance
that come from the word of God can, at times,
be challenging and forceful and more specific than
any multipronged human psychotherapy approach,
moving directly against and even separating between
ambivalence of thought and action, showing up
undesirable behaviors and the true nature
and intents of the mind.

****

Anchor Text Commentary from *Family Relational Health - A Biblical, Psycho-social Priority:* Chapter 6

The Conundrum of the Mind

If ever there was a conundrum, if ever there were mysteries, they would be the differing state and function of the relational mind. It simply cannot be understood. The mind is the core of our human existence, the very engine of our being, where our loving, our endearing marriage, parenting, and all other relationships are based and from which they operate. At the same time, it is equally the seat from which treachery, deception, and destruction arise and destroy relationships in the home and the entire society.

In therapy sessions, clients were seen displaying every manifestation from calm, composed, controlled, and reconciliatory emotions and behaviors to raw, unbridled, convulsive, and confrontational ones. What was heard and seen ranged from loving, affirming, assuring, consoling, and supportive expressions and embraces to demeaning, aggressive verbal abuses and physical altercations.

During these interventions, clients permitted, consented to, and cooperated with a deepening of the assessment into the folds and crevices of their family relational mind. Those surgical interventions sometimes had to be performed with a heavy dose of emotional anesthetic, such as comfort and care, assurance and reassurance, and prayer (for faith-based clients only and others if requested).

What was seen as a result of these interventions was the individual's inner thoughts, perspectives, and concepts of love, hatred, concerns, pride, shame, anger, guilt, desires, intentions, fears, hopes, despair, sensitivity, affection, bitterness, jealousy, trust, anxiety, and all the other relational emotions that were alive and active in both the conscious and subconscious chambers of the mind.

In summary of this conundrum, the following questions demand answers: Who can understand it? Who can explain the quandary and predicament of human relationships? In this state of bewilderment, confusion, and perplexity, humanity continues to struggle. Is there more to family life than problems, uncertainties, and ambiguities?

Remember: The above is an extract from Chapter 6. To get a clearer, deeper, fuller understanding and application of the text and topic, read the complete chapter in *Family Relational Health – A Biblical, Psycho-social Priority.*

Number 8: **Romans 12:2**
And be not conformed to this world:
but be ye transformed by the renewing of your mind,
that ye may prove what *is* that good, and acceptable,
and perfect, will of God

Paraphrased for Families
(Main Focus: the family in general)

*And do not continue practicing the old
patterns of relationships of this world
But improve them with a renewed healthy state of mind,
that you may experience that good and cherishable family
relationship which God intends for you
and which will prepare you and others
for the soon return of Christ.*

****

Anchor Text Commentary from *Family Relational Health - A Biblical, Psycho-social Priority*: Chapter 7

Transformation of the Mind

While we laud and applaud these and other groundbreaking scientific researches and exposés on these two issues of transformation and sensitivity, and their explanations on emotions and emotional behaviors, we are still going to be left lamenting and bewailing the gloomy fact that all evidence continues to point to the continuous deterioration of family relational health worldwide.

The masters and professors in our psychological, sociological, and anthropological communities have yet to come up with the winning formula to guarantee the positive change in behavior that will result in a stable, sustained quality of life in society. We are therefore forced to look for the answers from another source, and that source remains the Bible and its account of the origin of the species, not from Darwin's perspective but from the Creator Himself and His proffered answer to the human relational dilemma.

Body and Mind Transformation—Not the Same

Transforming *things?* Oh yes, definitely, we can! And we should point out that we have also mastered the skill of transforming sections of the human body. Cosmetic and plastic surgeries are heralded for making remarkable changes for good medical reasons as well as for persons who believe they need to be different for other reasons and motivations.

Transforming human beings from an undesirable social, behavioral, attitudinal, or mindset status is definitely not as easy, if at all possible. But such transformation is not only desirable but in many cases a dire and urgent need. It is undoubtedly one of the most far-reaching and influential endeavors that could be embarked upon in building a healthy, stable society.

What is it that makes this all-important work of transformation in human beings so daunting and apparently well-nigh impossible? It is the complexity and the mysterious nature of that aspect of human beings called the mind. Let us remind ourselves that one aspect of the foundation theory of family relational health is that all human relationships begin and continue to exist in the mind.

If the mind is so complex, mysterious, and well-nigh impossible to transform, then it goes without saying that the relationships that begin and continue to exist in it would understandably share the same state of complexity, mysteriousness, and difficulty to be transformed toward the desirable end.

We have also suggested that the mind is the avenue through which the Holy Spirit communicates with man. Only God, who knows the mind, can bring about any real lasting change to it. Our proposed solution to the family relational health dilemma includes transformation and getting rid of insensitivity and hypersensitivity in the mind. All of this can only be accomplished by the indwelling power of the Holy Spirit.

Remember: The above is an extract from Chapter 7. To get a clearer, deeper, fuller understanding and application of the text and topic, read the complete chapter in *Family Relational Health – A Biblical, Psycho-social Priority.*

Number 9: **Exodus 20:5–6**

Thou shalt not bow down thyself to them, nor serve them:
for I the LORD thy God am a jealous God,
visiting the iniquity of the fathers upon the children
unto the third and fourth generation of them that hate me;
And shewing mercy unto thousands of them that love me,
and keep my commandments.
Keeping mercy for thousands, forgiving
iniquity and transgression and sin,
and that will by no means clear the guilty;
visiting the iniquity of the fathers upon the children,
and upon the children's children,
unto the third and to the fourth generation.

Paraphrased for Families
(Main Focus: the family in general)

*Be aware that the quality of the relationship
that you have with Me, your God,
whether it be a loving one through obedience
or a hateful one through disobedience,
and consequently, the relationship that you
have with your family members,
have far-reaching effects and results
that do not end with your present family or generation.
It has the potential to impact many
more families and their offspring after you
and could even go on to influence your third
and fourth generations, long after you are gone.*

****

Anchor Text Commentary from *Family Relational Health - A Biblical, Psycho-social Priority:* Chapter 8

DNRA Anchor Statement

Successful human relationships *do not just happen!* The fairy-tale, magic wand-waving dream of "and they lived happily ever after!" with reference to marriage stops just where it began: that is, at it being a fairy tale! Nor does good parenting just happen. No human relationship becomes good by happenstance. Whether it is marriage, parenting, sibling, collegial, social, or any other human relationship, they are all influenced by more factors than those that meet the eyes.

It takes more than goodwill, good intention, and being a good Christian. One major factor that influences the quality of family relational health is a person's developmental notifiers of relational aptitude (DNRA).

DNRA Theory Background

Having established the objectives, let us look deeper at the basic concept of the DNRA. As each human being develops from conception into early adulthood (25–30 years of age), there are many signals that indicate the quality of the relationships that he or she will be able to forge and keep as he or she grows and matures. These signals, called *notifiers,* are based on the accumulated learning of the individual in the immediate family group, as well as from all others who influence his or her life directly and indirectly.

Let us consider five basic family relational health questions that will further stimulate interest in the study of the DNRA Theory:

1. Do you want to know how much your parents might have influenced or are presently influencing your state of mind and behavior and even your relationships?
2. Do you want to know the quality of the marital relationship that you might have if you are contemplating marriage?
3. Do you want to know the kind of parent you might become if you choose to have children?
4. Do you want to know why you behave the way you do at different times?

5. Do you want to know how your brothers, sisters, or other relatives might have influenced or are presently influencing you?

Most likely, the answers to the above questions are *yes*. We all want to know those facts. Unfortunately, the answers are not always as forthcoming as would be desired. In many cases, the questions are not even asked, or they might be pondered but not openly expressed.

To the same extent that we enquire into our family health ancestry and our personal health care history when we need a comprehensive medical assessment and treatment in order to establish where we are and how to proceed in our best interest, so it is equally important for our relational health that we address the ancestral and developmental issues raised in the above questions (CPH2).

Read Chapter eight in *Family Relational Health, A Biblical, Psycho-Social Priority,* to get a clearer understanding of the DNRA on our relationships.

Number 10: **Psalm 42:5**
Why art thou cast down, O my soul? and why art thou disquieted in me?
hope thou in God: for I shall yet praise him for the help of his countenance.

Paraphrased for Families
(Main Focus: the family in general)

Why am I feeling so low in spirit?
And why am I so depressed?
I do not have to be like this.
I can exercise hope in God and give praise to Him,
because His presence in me will inspire and brighten my mind.

****

Anchor Text Commentary from *Family Relational Health - A Biblical, Psycho-social Priority*: Chapter 9

Alienation from God

Among the many effects of sin on the human mind is the feeling of disconnection and despair. For different persons, this sense of utter alienation and disengagement can affect our relationships with all those around us and even with God. That is what David was experiencing when the Holy Spirit healed him and inspired him to make a record of that experience in the interest of others who would come after him and feel that way. "For whatsoever things were written aforetime were written for our learning, that we through patience and comfort of the scriptures might have hope" (Rom. 15:4).

The Holy Spirit had David record his gloomy and dark state of mind for the benefit of those who will go through similar moments in these days, so that they can have patience and hope. We are to have the assurance that such feelings do not mean that all is lost or that we have come to the end of life. It is simply human! Adam and Eve must have had their bouts of feelings of disconnection, detachment, and despair, all anchored in guilt and shame, as they sought to settle down to life outside of the Garden of Eden.

Until the full and complete restoration to the paradise experience in the Garden of Eden, we will have to do more than, as the song says, "go on singing." Until then, we have to live. Until then, we have to find the healthy way to relate with and manage the natural experiences of the "disturbing Ds": disconnection, discouragement, disquietude, dejection, despair, depression, detachment, disengagement, desperation, and despondency. These are the feelings of being laid bare, exposed, and vulnerable, as a result of sin on the mind.

Remember: The above is an extract from Chapter 9. To get a clearer, deeper and fullest understanding and application of the text and topic, read the complete chapter in *Family Relational Health – A Biblical, Psycho-social Priority.*

Number 11: **Psalm 139:14**

I will praise thee; for I am fearfully *and* wonderfully made:
marvellous *are* thy works; and *that* my soul knoweth right well.

Paraphrased for Families (1)
(Main Focus: the family in general)

I will give You praise always, Lord, because I know how whole and perfect You have made me. All of Your creation is filled with wonder and marvel. Above all is my intelligent mind, which knows well what is right in Your sight.

****

Anchor Text Commentary from *Family Relational Health - A Biblical, Psycho-social Priority:* Chapter 10

Wonderfully Made for Relationship

One key question we need to address is: What does our being "fearfully and wonderfully made" have to do with the subject of this book - family relational health? Of all the differences between the two main biological forms of animate life that God made, animals and human beings, the most outstanding is the human's ability to forge and keep relationships. That capability is the work of the active, sound mind which is akin to that of the Creator. The first understanding here is that God made man – male and female, to be in a relationship with Him.

Let us consult our Glossary for the working definition of *relationship:* The conscious process of ongoing intrapersonal awareness in one's mind, and the engagement of that conscious mind *with* or *against* another mind (interpersonal) in an effort to produce a desired result. This is based on the understanding that all human relationships begin and continue to exist in the active, sound mind. Once engagement of minds is established, the resulting relationship can be mostly and purposefully positive (with), or negative (against) and rarely ever neutral.

Active sound-mindedness is a physiological and psychological attribute that is unique to humans. David's inspiration led him to realize that in his *soul,* meaning his *mind,* he "knows well what is right in your sight." Nothing else in God's vast creation here on earth possesses that quality or characteristic of being - the relational mind.

God's CPRI: Differentiated Animal and Human Mind Consciousness

Let us go for some simple, clear, visible facts to substantiate that position.

1. God *called* the animals into being (Gen. 1:20–21, 24–25).
2. God *created/made* man instead (Gen. 1:26–27).
3. The creation of man was a consultation of Minds, those of the Godhead: Father, Son, and Holy Spirit: "Let *Us* make man" (Gen. 1:26).
4. God was intimate with man in that He breathed into the nostril of man (Gen. 2:7).

Fact 4 involves the first CPR (cardiopulmonary resuscitation) performed on earth. However, by virtue of the fact that man was not dead, having not yet come to life, the CPR act would be better seen as CPRI (Creator's procreative relationship initiative or Creator's personalized relationship initiative). This means that God's intimate act in bringing man (Adam and Eve separately) into being was the first demonstrable evidence of relationship-building.

God did not merely call them into being. He was divinely gregarious as He touched, made, and molded them. He was up close, upfront, and personal as He replicated Himself in this new being of His creation. This was God's love first performed on earth, an exemplary love which was to permeate the minds of all members of the human family who would come after, beginning with the marriage relationship.

Remember: The above is an extract from Chapter 10. To get a clearer, deeper and fullest understanding and application of the text and topic, read the complete chapter in *Family Relational Health – A Biblical, Psycho-social Priority.*

Number 12: **Ephesians 5:31–33**

For this cause shall a man leave his father and mother, and shall
be joined unto his wife, and they two shall be one flesh. This is
a great mystery: but I speak concerning Christ and the church.
Nevertheless, let every one of you in particular so love his wife even
as himself; and the wife see that she reverence her husband.

Paraphrased for Families (1)
(Main Focus: husbands and wives)

*When a man and a woman get married, with their hearts being joined as
husband and wife, ideally they individually should leave the overshadowing
and protection of their parents' homes and live their new life together as
one family. This is a mysterious experience, but it is beyond the mere union
of a man and a woman because God designed their human union to be
a symbol and object lesson of Christ joining Himself with the church so
that it becomes one with Him. However, in the marriage, it is important
that the husband especially loves his wife in the same way that he loves
himself, and the wife is to reciprocate with honor toward her husband.*

****

Anchor Text Commentary from *Family Relational
Health - A Biblical, Psycho-social Priority*: Chapter 10

The Mystery of the Marriage Relationship

With more emphasis on the mystery that Paul referred to in Ephesians,
we return to the first equation in what could be considered the
mysterious line in the topic of this chapter: $1 + 1 = 1$. That equation
evokes a simple question: How? It is not humanly and mathematically
correct. It is not normally or naturally correct, hence its mysterious
nature. So it is with God. He Himself is mysterious, and His ways are
past finding out (Rom. 11:33; see also Ps. 72:5, Isa. 40:28, and Eccl.
11:5), and that nature He has passed on, in part, to the human whom
He has made in His likeness.

But God, the designer of marriage, did not leave this mystery
of marriage totally inexplicable to His children. Seeing that the

relationship is the highest that the human can experience on earth (after their relationship with Him), God made provision to open man's relational mind to understand and thereby enjoy the bliss of that relationship. The quality of that marriage relationship between husband and wife, based on God's original divine plan, would set the tone, pace, and quality for all other relationships that would flow from it.

Those outflowing relationships would be the father-mother relationship, the parent-child relationship, the sibling relationship, and all the other multifaceted ones to emerge from these. This complex outworking itself is mysterious, and understandably so, to the mind that is not led by the Spirit of God (1 Cor. 2:14).

Remember : The above is an extract from Chapter 10. To get a clearer, deeper and fullest understanding and application of the text and topic, read the complete chapter in Book 1. *Family Relational Health – A Biblical, Psycho-social Priority.*

Number 13: **Genesis 3:16**

Unto the woman he said, I will greatly multiply thy sorrow and
thy conception; in sorrow thou shalt bring forth children; and thy
desire shall be to thy husband, and he shall rule over thee.

Paraphrased for Families (1) (Main Focus: husbands and wives)

*God explained to Eve: As a result of your yielding to the temptation of Satan,
the role of childbearing for which I have equipped your body is now going to be
uncomfortable and painful from conception to delivery, and further yet, because
you strayed from your husband into the temptation, you will need to seek his
permission and support for whatever major decisions you consider. And as a
result of your joint sin, your husband is going to laud his leadership over you.*

****

Anchor Text Commentary from *Family Relational Health - A Biblical, Psycho-social Priority*: Chapter 11

Did God Design Their Punishment?

There are many who interpret the pain that Adam and Eve, and
consequently all of us, their descendants, experience as a punishment
inflicted by God, based on the statement "*I will* greatly multiply thy
sorrow." We know that God is not a sadist; therefore, He takes "no
pleasure in the death of him that dieth" (Ezek. 18:32 and 33:11), and
therefore not in their pain either.

In the language of the Bible writers, every act is attributed to God,
without distinction between His designed will and His permissive
will. At the end of every major segment of His Creation, He declared
it was good (Gen. 1:4, 10, 12, and so on). Good is God's nature, and
He cannot be otherwise. At the same time, that same nature does not
condone or overlook sin. (Psa. 5: 4, Heb. 1: 13)

In His permitting it to run its consequential course, He is seen
as causing it to happen. But that is where the distinction between
causing, permitting, and *doing* comes in. In order to make the correct

attribution, we need to know and understand the character of God, and that is fully summed up in a simple but profound expression of the praise "God is good all the time, and all the time God is good, and that's His nature."

We can conclude that what God said to Adam and Eve was a description of what He saw and would permit, in love, to happen to them, as against it being a prescription of His for their punitive annihilation. It is a consequence that He would permit, but for which He would provide them with grace to endure (1 Cor. 10:13) until the fullness of the Protoevangelium is realized (Gen. 3:15).

Remember: The above is an extract from Chapter 11. To get a clearer, deeper and fullest understanding and application of the text and topic, read the complete chapter in Book 1. *Family Relational Health – A Biblical, Psycho-social Priority.*

Number 14: **1 Peter 3:7**

Likewise, ye husbands, dwell with them according to knowledge, giving honour unto the wife, as unto the weaker vessel, and as being heirs together of the grace of life; that your prayers be not hindered.

Paraphrased for Families (2)

(Main Focus: husbands and wives)

In the same way, you husbands, learn to relate with your wives with knowledge and understanding, showing honor and due respect to them, knowing that their makeup is different from yours, their being of a more delicate and comely nature (see Jeremiah 6:2).
At the end of it all, you are both to be recipients of God's grace. Be sure to follow this counsel so that your prayers will not go unanswered by God as a result of the way that you treat your wives.

****

Anchor Text Commentary from *Family Relational Health - A Biblical, Psycho-social Priority*: Chapter 11

All Is Not Lost

When a marriage that was supposed to be healthy gets so damaged and distorted, and one pulls away from the other, the two visible discordant individuals stand in the full view of all onlookers. The oneness becomes dismantled, fully divided, and two unhealthy individuals result from what was supposed to be one healthy couple whose equation would be $1 + 1 = 1$, that is to say: 1 happy spouse + 1 happy spouse = 1 happy couple. Unfortunately, in the scenario under observation it turns out to be the equation: $1 - 1 = 2$, that is to say, 1 hurting couple – I hurting spouse = 2 hurting spouses.

In their unfortunate case, marriage – mystery = misery. Clearly, there is the loss of the charming pull of the mystery of each other in their individual minds. Their individuality becomes commonplace, and the novelty of the newness that might have brought them together gets worn out. The novelty of the new was replaced with the routine of the regular, there was nothing more about each other to study, know, understand, desire, and cherish. Forcing them to stay together could be a miserable experience, save for divine intervention.

Ideally, the marriage should remain intact and the husband and wife should grow old gracefully together until death do them part. But where the mystery of sin had its toll on the marriage before natural death, they can experience healing, and even if the union is not restored, they can live honorably and civilly apart, still in the blessed hope of the second coming of Christ when He will make all things new. (Rev. 21: 5)

Remember: The above is an extract from Chapter11. To get a clearer, deeper and fullest understanding and application of the text and topic, read the complete chapter in Book 1. *Family Relational Health – A Biblical, Psycho-social Priority.*

Number 15: **1 Corinthians 10:13**
There hath no temptation taken you but such as is common to man:
but God is faithful, who will not suffer you
to be tempted above that ye are able;
but will, with the temptation, also make a way to escape,
that ye may be able to bear it.

Paraphrased for Families
(Main Focus: the family in general)

Be assured that there are no relational challenges
that you face that are unique to your family,
but that all such marital, parental, or other issues
are common to families everywhere.
But the God of Families is faithful
and will not leave your family to be hurt and
suffer beyond which you can endure
but will, with the relational challenges,
also provide His approved human professional way to help,
so that you may be able to manage and improve your relationships.

****

Anchor Text Commentary from *Family Relational Health - A Biblical, Psycho-social Priority*: Chapter 12

Successful Relationships: Mission Possible

Here is the paraphrase of Solomon's conclusion in the context of family relational health:

Let us hear the final discussion on family relational health: reverence the God of Families and give due obedience to Him, for this is our complete responsibility and accountability to Him. Remember all our human relationships will be judged by Him, inclusive of every secret and private one, whether they be healthy or unhealthy.

We reaffirm that God's biddings are His enablings. He says that good human relationships are possible because He has already put in place what we need to make it possible. Successful relationships are ours for the asking.

"And it shall come to pass, that before they call, I will answer; and while they are yet speaking, I will hear" (Isa. 65:24). Inasmuch as that prophecy was primarily focused on the life in the new earth, the blessing is available today. That is why Jesus gave the assurance in Luke 11:9–10.

And I say unto you, Ask, and it shall be given you; seek, and ye shall find; knock, and it shall be opened unto you. For every one that asketh receiveth; and he that seeketh findeth; and to him that knocketh it shall be opened.

God's assurance of successful marriages, parenting, and other forms of human relationships are not the same as granting us immunity from the harsh realities of this sinful life. The foundation of the assurance is "My grace is sufficient for thee" (2 Cor. 12:9) to keep you amid all the vicissitudes of life.

Remember: The above is an extract from Chapter 12 To get a clearer, deeper and fullest understanding and application of the text and topic, read the complete chapter in Book 1. *Family Relational Health – A Biblical, Psycho-social Priority.*

Number 16: **Romans 5:20**

Moreover the law entered,
that the offense might abound.
But where sin abounded,
grace did much more abound.

Paraphrased for Families
(Main Focus: the family in general)

*The presence of God's law,
which is the standard of His righteousness,
shows up the demonic offenses of the past committed in the mind.
But as many demons of the past that might be affecting you,
God's grace is much more available to cover them
and make you whole and free from their effects.*

****

Supportive Commentary from *Family Relational
Health - A Biblical, Psycho-social Priority:* Chapter 9

Healing from the Past: Regardless of Satan's Contention

Speaking of those who know of our past and will keep us living there, we consider two encounters recorded in Zechariah 3 and Jude 9. We are assured that all is not lost, regardless of the issues and challenges of our past life.

When God sets out to reward the faithful, Satan assumes the role of prosecutor to hold up any evidence of the past that he succeeded in leading them to do contrary to God's will. Here we see the chief demon, Satan, protesting that God's people should not be credited with eternal life. "And he shewed me Joshua the high priest standing before the angel of the LORD, and Satan standing at his right hand to resist him" (Zech. 3:1).

What was Satan's point of contention? Their past!

Now Joshua was clothed with filthy garments, and stood before the angel. And he answered and spake unto those that stood before him, saying, Take away the filthy garments from him. And unto him he said, Behold, I have caused thine iniquity to pass from thee, and I will clothe thee with change of raiment. (verses 3–4).

As human beings, they had challenges in their past lives. Look at Moses; he disobeyed the Lord and struck the rock instead of speaking as he was instructed. Hence, he could not enter the Promised Land and died at Mount Nebo (Deut. 32:48–52 and 34:4–6).

Then Paul captures and repeats Jesus's reaffirmation. "And he said unto me, My grace is sufficient for thee: for my strength is made perfect in weakness. Most gladly therefore will I rather glory in my infirmities, that the power of Christ may rest upon me" (2 Cor. 12:9).

Remember: The above is an extract from Chapter 9. To get the clearer, deeper and fullest understanding and application of the text and topic, read the complete chapter in Book 1. *Family Relational Health – A Biblical, Psycho-social Priority.*

Number 17: **1 Corinthians 7:12–17**

But to the rest speak I, not the Lord:
If any brother hath a wife that believeth not,
and she be pleased to dwell with him, let him not put her away.
And the woman which hath an husband that believeth not,
and if he be pleased to dwell with her, let her not leave him.
For the unbelieving husband is sanctified by the wife,
and the unbelieving wife is sanctified by the husband:
else were your children unclean; but now are they holy.
But if the unbelieving depart, let him depart.
A brother or a sister is not under bondage in such
cases: but God hath called us to peace.
For what knowest thou, O wife, whether
thou shalt save thy husband?
or how knowest thou, O man, whether thou shalt save thy wife?

Paraphrased for Families

(Main Focus: husbands and wives)

Now to the differing spouse I say,
"Where your spouse does not share the same spiritual life ideals as you,
and where his or her difference is not an issue of immorality,
and where he or she does not antagonize or
outrightly oppose your Christian ideals
and is prepared to love you and live with those standards of the Christian ideals,
you should not leave your spouse or get frustrated with him or her;
nor should you water down or lessen your taste or desire for the ideal.
Instead, equip yourself with the relational skills
to practice such ideals with or before him or her,
knowing fully well that by positively maintaining your
taste for, and practicing such ideals,
you could very well inspire your spouse to accept what you believe and uphold,
thereby enriching your marriage and ultimately
saving both of you for the Lord's return."

✳✳✳✳✳✳✳✳✳✳✳✳✳✳✳

Supportive Commentary from *Family Relational Health - A Biblical, Psycho-social Priority*: Chapter 7

Closet Self-Affirmation and Daily Renewal

Another very important reason for the daily renewal of the mind is the testimony that is offered to those in one's sphere of influence. The Christian's good, healthy lifestyle is not for himself alone. We ought to live and let others see us living. That in itself is a testimony to the power of the grace of the indwelling Christ.

Decades ago, the late Dr. Paul Freed, president and founder of Transworld Radio, Bonaire, in preaching about the importance of one's life testimony, said, "Even if I don't believe what he says, I like a man who believes what he says." A more succinct rendition of that statement is the more popular "I prefer to see a sermon than to hear one!" A renewed state of mind therefore maintains its responsibility to, and its potential influence on, others. It remains true in many instances that we are our neighbor's Bible.

Remember: The above is an extract from the Chapter 7. To get the clearer, deeper and fullest understanding and application of the text and topic, read the complete chapter in Book 1. *Family Relational Health – A Biblical, Psycho-social Priority.*

Number 18: **Ephesians 6:12**
For we wrestle not against flesh and blood, but against
principalities, against powers, against the rulers of the darkness
of this world, against spiritual wickedness in high places.

Paraphrased for Families
(Main Focus: the family in general, especially for men)

*For we wrestle not just against ordinary male marginalization and
low sense of personal development but against the subtle forces set a
destroying God's original intent, purpose, and position of the male in
life—Against the satanic forces of the unisex movement, homosexuality,
and abdication of the role of the male in the home and society.*

****

Supportive Commentary from *Family Relational Health - A Biblical, Psycho-social Priority:* Chapter 11

Sentenced to Hard Labor

God saw the sinful kaleidoscope of human action, and in mercy to them, He described the future as it would be in their individual situation and consequently as a couple and family. By describing it to them, He raised their awareness of the consequence of their sin and at the same time, lovingly preparing them for what was to come.

It is important to note that before He mentioned the gloom of despair that was about to descend upon them, He mentioned the bloom of hope that would come after. This is our exemplary, caring God and Father showing us how we should relate with the erring members of our families in the face of the imminent consequence of their wrongdoing. Hope is always the antidote for despair.

One of the most despicable signs of evidence of that effect on many men today is their abdication of their God-appointed roles as husbands and fathers. Their sense of responsibility has descended to an alarming depth, leaving bewildered wives and mothers strenuously bearing the burden of providing for the family and growing up the children singlehandedly.

Many children have been deprived of their sense of paternal and family identity, resulting in truancy and maladaptive and maladjusted youngsters. In so many cases, the vicious cycle continues, especially with boys growing up without the example of good, responsible husbands and fathers. They are deprived of the needed demonstration of establishing care and providing for a family. Many end up drifting into the hands and arms of unscrupulous fellow men who themselves are victims of the same situation, and they forge relationships that are detestable and totally against nature. And many are those others who end up in hotbeds of crime and violence.

Painfully, so many of these otherwise potentially good young men seem to mount the same horse and ride down the same road of absenteeism and irresponsibility. Here we have a partial fulfillment of the prophecy by Ezekiel. "The fathers have eaten sour grapes, and the children's teeth are set on edge?" (Ezek. 18:2).

Girls have not escaped the ills of the absence of positive, healthy, father figures in their lives. Unwanted and teenage pregnancies and immoral lifestyles of many young women are the result of their not having the early exposure to the one who is supposed to be the first man in their lives: their father. From him, she should see how a healthy husband-father cares for his wife and children.

Remember: The above is an extract from Chapter 11. To get the clearer, deeper and fullest understanding and application of the text and topic, read the complete chapter in Book 1. *Family Relational Health – A Biblical, Psycho-social Priority.*

Number 19: **Genesis 1:27–28**

So God created man in his *own* image, in the image of God created he him; male and female created he them. And God blessed them, and God said unto them, Be fruitful, and multiply, and replenish the earth

Extrapolated and Paraphrased for Families
(Main Focus: the family in general)

I, your God, have no more plan to make
anymore of you directly with My own hands,
because I have entrusted and empowered you
with a small portion of My procreative power
to continue for Me where I have stopped in making you two.
So go ahead and populate the earth with your kind,
according to My original plan for your family.

****

Supportive Commentary from *Family Relational Health - A Biblical, Psycho-social Priority*: Chapter 8

Holy Sexual Procreation Plan—Conceived in the Mind of God

Adam and Eve's children were conceived after the Fall. Their sexual relationship, which resulted in Eve's pregnancy, was in harmony with God's plan for procreation. That was not sin. However, with their minds having been corrupted by sin, and consequently the whole being, the children were the products of their sinful bodies.

The procreation plan and method (sexual intercourse), having been conceived in the mind of God, remained holy, but unfortunately it had to be carried out in no-longer-holy vessels, His now-sinful children. He still kept them in the scheme of the procreation plan and initiated the redemption plan The Protoevangelium as His rescue mission for them (Gen. 3:15; John 3:16; Rev. 13:8; 1 Peter 1:20).

Against this fact, their children were indeed "shapen in iniquity; and in sin did their mother conceive them" (Ps. 51:5, paraphrased).

But the children were not without hope. Inasmuch as each child was born sinless, being born of sinful parents and inheriting the genes therefrom, they had the predisposed propensity and proclivity to sin and were therefore born with the need for a Savior. As the sinful nature began to be acted out in their minds and lives, the Holy Spirit balanced that experience by activating their sense of the need for the Savior as they grew more and more conscious of good and evil, right and wrong. (See John 10: 8)

Remember: The above is an extract from Chapter 8. To get the clearer, deeper and fullest understanding and application of the text and topic, read the complete chapter in Book 1. *Family Relational Health – A Biblical, Psycho-social Priority.*

Number 20: **James 1:5**

If any of you lack wisdom, let him ask of God, that giveth to all
men liberally, and upbraideth not; and it shall be given him.

Paraphrased for Families
(Main Focus: the family in general)

*If you know that you lack the relational skills for quality
Relationship and you genuinely desire to have them,
then ask of the God of Families,
Who will freely provide the means for you to get those skills
and will not rebuke you for asking?
Rest assured that you will get what you need*

****

Supportive Commentary from *Family Relational Health - A Biblical, Psycho-social Priority*: Chapter 6

Knowledge: God's Replacement Therapy for Family Ignorance

In an effort to destroy those forces that will incite, instigate, or engage in unhealthy relationships among His people, God provides a replacement therapy in order to stabilize and strengthen those relational minds. Through His inspired Word, He shows the positive state of mind that will influence quality, steadfast relationships to be experienced firstly in the home, the Church, and then in society.

He speaks through James: "If any of you lack wisdom, let him ask of God, that giveth to all men liberally, and upbraideth not; and it shall be given him. But let him ask in faith, nothing wavering. For he that wavereth is like a wave of the sea driven with the wind and tossed. For let not that man think that he shall receive any thing of the Lord. A double minded man is unstable in all his ways." (James 1: 5-8)

Here we see God alluding to the issue of ignorance which can have untold negative effects on family relationships. In this treatment plan, God expresses an invitation to all family members to ask Him for wisdom as Solomon did. He assures them that He will supply it liberally. In Isaiah 1:18–19, He sought to arrest the mind and invites us to reason with Him in an effort to heal a broken relationship: "Come now, and let us reason together, saith the Lord: though your sins be as scarlet, they shall be as white as snow; though they be red like crimson, they shall be as wool."

If ye be willing and obedient, ye shall eat the good of the land." Once the relationship between us and God is healthy, and we allow Him to separate us from the forces of evil that impair our relationships, we will succeed. That is the goal, and it is fully achievable though Him who gives us the victory. (Romans 7: 25)

Remember: The above is an extract from Chapter 6. To get the clearer, deeper and fullest understanding and application of the text and topic, read the complete chapter in Book 1. *Family Relational Health – A Biblical, Psycho-social Priority.*

Number 21: Ecclesiastes 12:17
Let us hear the conclusion of the whole matter: Fear God, and
keep his commandments: for this is the whole duty of man

Paraphrased for Families
(Main Focus: the family in general)

Let us hear the final discussion on family relational health.
Reverence the God of Families and give due obedience to Him
for this is our complete responsibility and accountability to Him.
Remember all our human relationships will be judged by Him,
inclusive of every secret and private one,
whether they be healthy or unhealthy.

****

Supportive Commentary from *Family Relational Health - A Biblical, Psycho-social Priority*: Chapter 12

Solomon's Epilogue on Life's Relationships

After looking at the wide panorama of life and reviewing the escapades he had gone through, Solomon, under inspiration, wrote what is regarded in many circles, both Christian and non-Christian, as the most profound, authoritative summary of life in the book of Ecclesiastes. Solomon's life was a real example of a conundrum, as he experienced the extremes of the ups and downs and ins and outs of risk-taking, exploratory, and audacious living.

At the end of that checkered, colorful life, God's original promise to Solomon prevailed. His wisdom outshone his foolish, disreputable life. Here is his epilogue on his adventures as he concluded his discourse on life, stated in his simple yet profound, characteristic manner:

Let us hear the conclusion of the whole matter: Fear God, and keep his commandments: for this is the whole duty of man. For God shall bring every work

into judgment, with every secret thing, whether it be
good, or whether it be evil. (Eccles.12:13–14)

Let us borrow from Solomon's wide experience and draw a
conclusion on our discourse in this book. If we want healing from
the relational issues, challenges, problems, and ultimately illnesses
of life, we must go to the original source, the fountain that God has
provided. All our efforts will continue to yield but little if we continue
to reject the counsels, guidelines, admonitions, and directives from
the One who made the relational mind.

Remember: The above is an extract from Chapter 12. To get the
clearer, deeper and fullest understanding and application of the text
and topic, read the complete chapter in Book 1. *Family Relational
Health – A Biblical, Psycho-social Priority.*

Number 22: **Joshua 24: 15**
"And if it seem evil unto you to serve the LORD,
choose you this day whom ye will serve;
whether the gods which your fathers served
that were on the other side of the flood,
or the gods of the Amorites, in whose land ye dwell:
but as for me and my house, we will serve the LORD."

Paraphrased for Families
(Main Focus: the family in general)

*You family leaders, make your choice today about the path on which you and
your families will go, whether following the patterns of the acclaimed social icons
of this world as many of your past and present family members have done and are
doing; or you will uphold the simple ideals of God's original family life. My family
and I have chosen to lovingly obey what God has established for us to follow.*

****

Supportive Commentary from *Family Relational Health – A
Biblical, Psycho-social Priority:* Chapter 4 & Appendix 3

The Power of Choice: Man's Only Real Possession

A brief review reminds us that at Creation, God made a perfect man
with conditional immortality subject to his loving obedience to his
Creator. Man's mind was perfect and had the power of choice, which
up to this day, is the only personal possession any human being has.
Even his thoughts are not truly his own! They are either inspired by the
indwelling Holy Spirit or motivated by the impressions on the mind
by the warring, opposing evil forces around us. The power of choice
is all that we have to determine which side we prefer: the side of God
and His righteousness, or the side of Satan and his unrighteousness.

God started off Adam and Eve with a perfect mind through which
He was to maintain communion between them. They chose the route
of disobedience and unrighteousness, and their minds consequently

became tainted and damaged by sin. But as we have already noted above through John, God never gave up on them.

Following God's pattern, family members ought to cultivate and practice the spirit of forgiveness and reconciliation. "And forgive us our debts, as we forgive our debtors" (Matt. 6:12). No one has the right to hold a hard end against the other, bearing in mind that the forgiver today might need to be the forgiven tomorrow.

Exemplary State Leadership in Family Relational Health

Maybe one of the most current cases of diametrically opposite experience is that of the politically challenged British Prime Minister, Boris Johnson. A national outcry against him, demanding his resignation (2022) came against his failure as leader to abide by the Covid19 protocols and lockdown directives imposed under his leadership on the citizens (2020). This happened when he joined in a garden party at 10 Downing Street, the state residence from which the highest example should be sent to the nation.

There was such a time also in Joshua's leadership experience of Israel when he felt that he was confronting a free and laissez-faire society, even among the people of God. Then he threw down the gauntlet and spoke as every man who is in charge of his household ought to do, even today: "And if it seem evil unto you to serve the LORD, choose you this day whom ye will serve; whether the gods which your fathers served that were on the other side of the flood, or the gods of the Amorites, in whose land ye dwell: but as for me and my house, we will serve the LORD" (Josh. 24:15).

Quality family relational health for society will continue to be a controversial and potentially divisive issue. What will be acceptable to determine how relationally healthy families are or need to be? It seems to come down to the very opposite of what happened in Nineveh: Each one, each family or household leader along with the members thereof, will determine what their standards of acceptable behavior and operations will be. A complete and totally free and open society. ...

However, for the Christian family, it must be according to Joshua's position: We will order our lives in accordance with that which pleases the Lord, our God of Families. Our family relational health vital signs will be directed by the inspiration of the Lord and will be devised, constructed, taught, and administered by His appointed leaders in harmony with His instructions.

Remember: The above is an extract from Chapter 4 and Appendix 3. To get the clearer, deeper and fuller understanding and application of the text and topic, read the complete chapter and appendix in Book 1 of *Family Relational Health – A Biblical, Psycho-social Priority.*

Number 23: **Isaiah 54:2**
Enlarge the place of thy tent,
and let them stretch forth the curtains of thine habitations:
spare not, lengthen thy cords,
and strengthen thy stakes.

Paraphrased for Families
(Main Focus: husbands and wives)

*Expand the influence and inspiration of your marital relationship,
and let its effect be felt on those in your sphere of influence;
spare no effort to improve, increase the positive impact of your spousal bond,
and fortify your relational anchors even to the benefit of those around you.*

****

Supportive Commentary from *Family Relational Health - A Biblical, Psycho-social Priority*: Chapter 5

Marriage Under Attack

We hear "Marriage is under attack!" and the rallying call is for us to "fight back." *Us* here means the entire Church community, married and unmarried, men and women, young and elderly, and everyone in between. Understandably, those who are married are to be in the forefront of the battle, because each couple (husband and wife) has their own marriage to save. But the entire Church ought to have a vested interest in the well-being of the marriages that are in it, because marriage, correctly understood according to Genesis 2:24, is the foundation of the family, and according to Ephesians 5, it is an extension of the teaching of the Gospel.

God uses the marriage relationship as a symbol of His relationship with His people (Jer. 3:14). Marriage was the first human institution that God created in the Garden of Eden (Gen. 2:21–25). It was in response to the first marital issue that the protoevangelium (the first proclamation of the Gospel) was made (Gen. 3:15). And it was at a marriage ceremony that Jesus performed His first miracle (John 2:1–11).

What more assurance could the Church need that the marital relationship is of top priority of all human relationships to God? Little wonder that it is Satan's primary target. Remember the hurricane-earthquake analogy in chapter 2: destroy the foundation and the superstructure will crumble to the ground.

Remember: To get a wider understanding of the developing complexities and diversities of family and their subsequent, potential impact on marriage, read the entire Extrapolations 5 and 6 from Chapter 5 of Book 1. *Family Relational Health – A Biblical, Psychosocial Priority.*

Number 24: **Psalm 34:8**
O taste and see that the LORD is good:
blessed is the man that trusteth in him.

Paraphrased for Families
(Main Focus: husbands and wives)

Oh, taste and see that marriage is still good!
Blessed is the couple and family who trusts in the Lord,
and whose lives can testify to others looking on, that it is so.

****

Supportive Commentary from *Family Relational Health -*
A Biblical, Psycho-social Priority: Chapters 10

Mystery of the Marriage Relationship (Extended)

Keeping the focus of the mysterious mathematical equation on the two individuals around whom it is constructed, that is the husband and the wife, let us see its immediate application in the context of their being fearfully and wonderfully made. To do this, let us review ten of the general, basic facts about them as spouses, individually:

1. They were born separately.
2. He is male; she is female.
3. They were born to different parents.
4. Their location, community, nationality, and culture could be quite different in more ways than one.
5. While there are commonalities with their biology and physiology, there are equally stark differences—skeletally, structurally, and in some instances, anatomically, hormonally, and chemically.
6. Their temperaments and personalities can be distinct and separate.
7. Their mind-processing of the same issue can be patently different and even opposite at times.

8. Their ordinary tastes, desires, likes, and dislikes, among many others personal dynamics, could be palpably different.
9. Their internal family culture and practices can be not only different but potentially diverse.
10. Their perspectives, outlook on life, and consequently worldview could also be not only different but potentially diverse.

Just a cursory nonclinical glance at this list of differences between potential spouses in the intended marriage is enough to boggle the mind! How can they live happily committed together in love and harmony for one, five, ten, twenty, forty, sixty, and even more years, until death do them part? That is clearly a mysterious goal. But again, as we repeat in this book, God's biddings are His enablings. He bids it, He says it is possible, and therefore it is. The possibility of this accomplishment lies in the very key word that describes the relationship: mystery.

Here we see that $1 + 1 = 1$ works out to be what Jesus said in Matthew 19:5, that at marriage the two are no longer two but one. This oneness takes place in their minds before it is demonstrated in their bodies. Their two minds are mysteriously bonded in one, while maintaining their distinct individuality. Here the two exemplify the mysterious Godhead, three distinct persons—the Father, Son, and Holy Spirit.

This is the Trinity, the three-in-one God that distinguished them (the Godhead) from polytheism that the Israelites were exposed to, in their four hundred years of slavery in Egypt. That is why He instructed Moses to teach that as one of their first post-slavery lessons on their way to freedom of worship en-route to the Promised Land. "Hear, O Israel: The LORD our God is one LORD: And thou shalt love the LORD thy God with all thine heart, and with all thy soul, and with all thy might" (Deuteronomy 6:4–6; see also Mark 12:29).

Remember: The above is an extract from Chapter 10. To get the clearer, deeper and fullest understanding and application of the text and topic, read the complete chapter in Book 1. *Family Relational Health – A Biblical, Psycho-social Priority.*

Number 25: **Ephesians 4:28**
Let no corrupt communication proceed out of your mouth,
but that which is good to the use of edifying,
that it may minister grace unto the hearers.

Paraphrased for Families
(Main Focus: the family in general)

*Let the relational expressions that you make
be of a healthy nature, so that you can be positively spontaneous,
uninhibited, unreserved, unconditional, and confidently vulnerable in everything
that you say, thus making you able to edify and equip each other with relational
skills to grow in love and glorify the God of human relationships.*

****

Supportive Commentary from *Family Relational Health - A Biblical, Psycho-socia Priority:* Introduction & Chapter 6

Family Relational Health and a Good Christian Life

If a family member does not make the necessary efforts, if such a person does not seek to equip him or herself with family relational skills in order to improve the quality of the relationship between him or herself and the significant others in his or her life, then that neglect would be considered a refusal to improve his or her family relational health.

Rapport: One of the four vital signs of *family relational health* anchored in the cognitive and affective domains of the mind. It produces the sense of reciprocal communication between family members for mutual benefit. This vital sign reflects the combined action of the intelligence (cognitive) and the affective (feeling) in the way that verbalization or relational expressions are made.

God Made the Human Mind

Our first bewildering question about the human relational mind is, "Who can understand it?" The Bible clearly states that God can. First of all, He made man after His own image and into His own likeness (Gen. 1:26–27). The image and likeness were not just in the form and structure of the created being but more so in his mind.

God made the mind as the channel through which communication and relationship between Him and His children would be established, maintained, and developed ad-infinitum. God also gave them (male and female) the power of choice and the opportunity to align their minds individually with His through loving obedience (Gen. 2:15–17).

Remember: The above is an extract from Chapter 6. To get the clearer, deeper and fullest understanding and application of the text and topic, read the complete chapter 6 in Book 1. *Family Relational Health – A Biblical, Psycho-social Priority.*

Number 26: **Proverbs 6:6**
Go to the ant, thou sluggard;
consider her ways, and be wise.

Paraphrased for Families
(Main Focus: the family in general)

*Go to the sheep under attack,
you vulnerable family members,
observe how they bond tightly together
when they are attacked by wolves or dingoes,
and in unity help to save each other.
Do likewise, and you shall defeat the onslaught of
the enemies of healthy family life.*

****

Supportive Commentary from *Family Relational Health - A Biblical, Psycho-social Priority*: Chapter 5

Acceptable Time for Family Reunion

Given that both the original Bible-based family structure and God's ideal for family life are fiercely and relentlessly being attacked, now is the time for healthy family reunion.

In sheep-rearing countries like Australia, one of greatest predators of the sheep is the dingo or the fox. Some of these predators set the field for an attack by going on a high rock within jumping proximity to the sheep, and then it gives out a blood-curdling roar!

The strategy is that the roar will immobilize the timid, fainthearted flock and make it easy for an attack. Indeed, the strategy does work, but only in part. The weak, terrified sheep, in panic and shock, huddle so tightly together so that when the enemy makes the victory jump and dash upon them, it ends up with a mouthful of wool instead of flesh because of the tight closeness into which the sheep bond themselves.

Dysfunctional Families—Fodder for the Enemy

A dysfunctional, broken family relationship is fodder in the hands of the forces united to destroy God's original family blueprint. When families, especially those in the Church, are disjointed and fractured, they give ample evidence to the adversaries to prove their point that the traditional family ideals have failed. Therefore, they argue that any form, structure, type, or combination that works is just as good, as long as the parties have a meaningful relationship.

It is unfortunate and even regrettable that in today's society, the practice of family reunion is observed only on holidays. We cannot make light of the beauty and great purpose of such occasions. As a result of migration for different purposes and sound reasons, family members do look forward to such times of reunion, and they need to be encouraged. However, the well-being and healthy family bonding should not be left only to such times, especially when efforts can be made to do better.

Remember: The above is an extract from Chapter 5. To get the clearer, deeper and fullest understanding and application of the text and topic, read the complete chapter in Book 1. *Family Relational Health – A Biblical, Psycho-social Priority.*

Number 27: **1 Corinthians 11:26**
For as often as ye eat this bread, and drink this cup,
ye do shew the Lord's death till he come.

Paraphrased for Families
(Main Focus: the family in general)

*As often as you have healthy family reunions
that positively strengthen your earthly family ties,
you do show your preparedness for the grand
family reunion of all the ages, when the Lord returns.*

****

Supportive Commentary from *Family Relational
Health - A Biblical, Psycho-social Priority*: Chapter 5

Two New Types of Family Reunion

Every day ought to be a family reunion experience. There are at least two major reunion experiences that each family can have daily. Let us consider them.

Daily Family Reunion 1: Waking Up in the Morning

The first stanza of a well-loved morning hymn by John Keble (1792–1866) reads,

> New every morning is thy love, Our waking and
> uprising prove, Through sleep and darkness safely
> brought, Restored to life and power and thought.
> (From his poem "Hues of the Rich Unfolding
> Morn," Hymntime.com)

During the hours of sleep, although some might be sleeping in the same bed, they are technically separated. The sleep experience is as individual as death, such that Jesus made a close comparison between the two, using Lazarus as the point of reference (John 11:11–14).

There are countless times when two family members go to sleep and only one awakens the next morning. The other failed to reunite, as he or she goes off into the permanent sleep, awaiting the resurrection.

All who pass through the darkness of night and reappear in the light of the new day together should see that reunion as a cause for praise to God and a recommitment to the well-being of each other. That is the purpose of family morning devotion. It serves the purpose of relinking us together and with God.

Daily Family Reunion 2: Returning Home

When family members have to leave home for work or school, or any other place, especially for an extended period, the time of separation from home can be filled with anxiety, hope, and even concern for each other's safety and well-being. They look forward to their reunion. Sometimes they text and call each other, enquire about their mutual welfare, and express longing for the one who is away to return home. They look forward to sharing experiences of what happened in and outside of the home.

In a healthy relationship, these reunions have esteemed value, and in a definite way, they strengthen the bond that keeps the family strong. (See Song Numbers 49 & 51)

Remember: The above is an extract from Chapter 5. To get the clearer, deeper and fullest understanding and application of the text and topic, read the complete chapter in Book 1. *Family Relational Health – A Biblical, Psycho-social Priority.*

Number 28: **1 Corinthians 15:33**

Be not deceived:
evil communications corrupt good manners.

Paraphrased for Families
(Main Focus: the family in general)

Do not be fooled:
if you become involved in a relationship
with a questionable or evil person,
your good qualities can be compromised
and you become like that person.
Be aware!

****

Supportive Commentary from *Family Relational Health - A Biblical Psycho-social Priority*: Chapters 8

Human Relationships Have Far-Reaching Influence

About 80 percent of our lives are influenced by our relationships, whether marital, parental, sibling, sororal/fraternal, social, or business/transactional. In professional premarital counseling, emphasis is placed on the importance of carefully choosing one's life partner, because he or she will have a virtual lifelong influence on the quality of the other's life.

The proverbial statement "Show me your company (relationships) and I will tell you who you are," is a fact of life affirmed by the wise man Solomon. "He that walketh with wise men shall be wise: but a companion of fools shall be destroyed" (Prov. 13:20). Late US Air Force Chaplain Ronnie Melancon (1942-2021) renders it this way: "Show me your friends and I'll show you your future."

The apostle Paul adds his counsel regarding the impact associates can have on us. "Be not deceived: evil communications corrupt good manners" (1 Cor. 15:33). Paraphrased with direct application to family relational health, the text might read, "Do not be fooled. If you become involved in a relationship with a questionable or evil person, your good qualities can be compromised and you become like that person. Be aware!"

Two Key Pointers

1 Be conscious of the company and relationships you cherish. Aim to shed negative influences always, and be alert and do not allow any unhealthy influence to overpower your mind.

2 Guard well the thoughts of your mind and carefully watch your utterances. It is not your tongue that is the source of what you say wrong or incorrectly; it is your mind from which the utterances are generated.

Remember: The above is an extract from Chapter 8. To get the clearer, deeper and fullest understanding and application of the text and topic, read the complete chapter in Book 1. *Family Relational Health – A Biblical, Psycho-social Priority.*

Number 29: **Hebrews 4:8–9**

For if Jesus had given them rest, then would he not afterward have spoken of another day. There remaineth therefore a rest to the people of God.

Paraphrased for Families
(Main Focus: the family in general)

For if God had made or intended any change to be made in His originally ascribed roles of the male and the female, the man and the woman, the husband and the wife, in the operations of the family at home and by extension the extended assembled family in the church/temple, would He not afterward have inspired and instructed that such change be made? There remains therefore the original healthy operational and leadership plan for the family as God established it at creation and consistently affirmed it down through the ages. Let us therefore be careful and wary of any convenient misinterpretation or change to God's original design, lest it renders us unable to enjoy good relational health in the family at home and at church and failure to enter the future family home when Jesus returns.

****

Supportive Commentary from *Family Relational Health - A Biblical, Psycho-social Priority*: Chapter 11

Satan, the Master Divider

Although it is just the two of us—male and female, man and woman—who were fearfully and wonderfully made at Creation, not with sameness or uniformity but with complementary and complimentary equality, the ideal goal of sustained harmonious coexistence has yet to be realized. The house, and consequently the home, have become and have remained divided.

Not only is Satan the master divider in the human family (beginning in Eden), but he is also the master manipulator. His strategy is to divide and conquer by pitting one family member against the other. He inspired separation, distrust, and disloyalty, then manipulated them into the blame game and then into rivalry. That is the genesis of the relational debacle between the two sexes.

With the deterioration over time, it has now become known as the culturally and socially based gender battle or the battle of the sexes. This we believe subtly accounts for the feminist movement. Good and plausible as it appears on the surface, it is unhealthy in its depth, strategy, and ultimate outcome. The ultimate outcome of the movement is the infighting and wrangling and power struggle of the genders. It is the classic case of the pendulum being swung from one extreme to the other.

Rivalry between the sexes and the evolving imbalance as a result of the social characterization of the roles and expectations of the sexes, were not a part of God's plan for the human family. To the same extent, it was not His plan to have more focus placed on our physiological health, the state and function of the body, at the expense of the psychological, the state and function of the mind (CPH^2).

Being fearfully and wonderfully made meant that symmetry and purposeful balance would be maintained as the hallmark of healthy development of both male and female, as exemplified in Jesus's growth and development (Luke 2:52).

The above was a short extract from Chapter 11. To get the clearer, deeper and fullest understanding and application of the text and topic, read the complete chapter in Book 1. *Family Relational Health – A Biblical, Psycho-social Priority.*

Number 30: **Genesis 1:27**
So God created man in his own image,
in the image of God created he him;
male and female created he them.

Paraphrased for Families
(Main Focus: the husband-father and wife-mother
and extending to the family in general)

*So God created the man and the woman in His own image and blessed
their active, sound relational minds with the ability to forge and keep
a healthy, multifunctional, and unbiased family relationship with each
individual member in their household, similarly to how He maintains
such individual relationship with all His children on earth.*

****

Supportive Commentary from *Family Relational Health - A Biblical, Psycho-social Priority*: Chapter 10

God's Multifunctional Mind Implanted in Man

The Unfathomable Relational Mind

The intricate, complex, and mysterious combination and coordination of mind, soul, spirit, and conscience make up the *relational mind*, which David succinctly describes as *marvellous*. It is unfathomable because it is made by the Creator, Who is omnipotent, omniscient, omnipresent, and eternal. He simply cannot be explained.

This same Creator challenged one of His faithful children, Job: "Canst thou by searching find out God? Canst thou find out the Almighty unto perfection?" (Job 11:7). The answer is simply, and profoundly, No! It should be understood, then, that the part of His creation that is closest to Himself, man, would have been made a close representation of His own unfathomable and incomprehensible nature, so that not even the man can understand himself. Outside of God, and within himself by himself, man can do nothing. (John 15:5).

Let us now apply this exemplary caring relationship of God to the human family and relational health. To do this, we will compose a partial paraphrase of God's procreational command to the first family in the Garden of Eden. "So God created man in His own image, and blessed his mind with the ability to forge and keep a healthy, multifunctional family relationship with all those in his household" (Gen. 1:27).

Interpreted, this means that to the same extent that God in His omnipotence and omniscience can keep a healthy relationship with all His children, He has equipped the human mind with an adequate portion of His multi-relational power to forge and keep healthy relationships with all those in his sphere of influence, beginning with those in his household.

This explains how a man who is led by the God of Families can multifunction as a good man, a faithful husband, a caring father for as many children as his quiver can hold (Ps. 127:5), and a supporter of other relatives and still identify with the life of the community and therefore be seen as a model citizen. This is all possible because of his relationship with God, from whom he draws relational skills to help in his time of need (Heb. 4:16).

Remember : The above is an extract from Chapter 10. To get the clearer, deeper and fullest understanding and application of the text and topic, read the complete chapter in Book 1. *Family Relational Health – A Biblical, Psycho-social Priority.*

Number 31: **1 Corinthians 11:26**
For as often as ye eat this bread, and drink this cup,
ye do shew the Lord's death till he come.

Paraphrased for Families
(Main Focus: husbands and wives)

For as often as you engage your mind and share your body in holy, mutual,
healthy sexual intercourse (Hebrews 13:4), you do show your love for each other,
affirming My original marital plan and bonding yourselves together until I come.

****

Supportive Commentary from *Family Relational*
Health - A Biblical, Psycho-social Priority: Chapter 11

Eve's Dependence upon Adam

For Eve, (and subsequently all women), one of the consequence of sin would be pain in childbirth. "Unto the woman he said, I will greatly multiply thy sorrow and thy conception; in sorrow thou shalt bring forth children (Gen. 3:16, first part). The throes and travails of delivery would range from uncomfortable to excruciating. And even before those, there would be the nauseated feelings (morning sickness), the potential spike in blood pressure, her body falling out of shape, among other experiences. Her female and childbearing hormones, such as estrogen and progesterone, would not always be at their normal levels. They would begin their fearful manifestation in menarche and could even get worse if she becomes the victim of dysmenorrhea (painful monthly periods).

Her gynaecological and obstetric body functions, the calibration during the nine-month gestation period, and the experience at delivery would not go as they were designed before the Fall. Twelve times in the King James Version of the Bible have her pain and anguish been referred to analogically to emphasize that sin is, by all account, intolerable: "For I have heard a voice as of a woman in travail, and the anguish as of her that bringeth forth her first child ..." (Jer. 4:31).

Then there would be the natural dependence on her husband for support, including the feeling of security and protection that she will truly need, but which unfortunately might not be forthcoming as she desires and deserves: "... and thy desire shall be to thy husband, and he shall rule over thee" (Genesis 3:16, last part).

Eve would undoubtedly have symptoms of posttraumatic stress disorder (PTSD) from the negative flashbacks of her encounter with the serpent, as she had to grapple with the painful consequences. There would also be guilt feelings from the reminder from her husband that they are going through those difficulties because of her weakness in yielding to the temptation of the evil one.

The negative back-and-forth of verbal accusations, emotional alienation, her occasional disillusionment, and constant unfulfilled expectations will weaken her sense of self-esteem and weigh her down. Not least among these times of disillusionment will be her sense of unfulfilled sexual desire and satisfaction. Look again at the paraphrase of anchor text 1 at the beginning of the chapter.

Given the biological and physiological complexity of her sexual physiology over that of her husband, including her much lower level of the sex libido hormone, testosterone, and given his ignorance of such facts and his own impatience and inexperience, she could end up feeling sexually frustrated and even used by him at times. Thus, her desires will be, to her husband in so many ways, not dictated and inflicted by God, but by the sinful falling out of the natural, healthy circuitry of their relational minds.

Remember : The above is an extract from Chapter 11. To get the clearer, deeper and fullest understanding and application of the text and topic, read the complete chapter in Book 1. *Family Relational Health – A Biblical, Psycho-social Priority.*

Number 32: **Hebrews 4:15**

For we have not an high priest which cannot be touched with the feeling of our infirmities; but was in all points tempted like as we are, yet without sin.

Paraphrased for Families
(Main Focus: the family in general)

We are assured that Jesus, our Wonderful Counselor (Isaiah 9:6), understands the positive effect of countertransference and self-disclosure so that He, having been truly human while here among us, can truly say, "I understand." ("I've been there, done that!) And because He experienced it as fully human, if you allow Him now to infuse your mind via His Spirit, He will empower you to experience the same victory that He had over every temptation.

****

Supportive Commentary from *Family Relational Health - A Biblical, Psycho-social Priority*: Chapter 12

God's Biddings Are His Enablings

He says that marriage can work successfully, until death do they part, and it has happened, is happening, and will continue to happen until Christ comes the second time. He says that despite the failure of multitudes of parents, as in the case of Priest Eli (1 Sam. 2:28–36 and 3:11–14), effective parenting and parent-child relationships are still possible today and will continue to be realized even to His coming.

Let us emphasize a salient point. Our conviction and persuasion about God's biddings being His enablings is based on the guarantee and assurance in His word, because He cannot lie (Titus 1:2). He says, "And he said unto me, My grace is sufficient for thee: for my strength is made perfect in weakness. Most gladly therefore will I rather glory in my infirmities, that the power of Christ may rest upon me" (2 Cor. 12:9).

There is also the supporting fact for that conviction based on our understanding of how He created us. It is He who made the human relational mind, akin to His having made man in His own image. He equipped and fortified the mind with the inherent skills and ability to forge and keep healthy relationships. Conditions applied, however. They would only be able to experience success in their relationships as long as they would be willing to abide in Him and follow His guidance and instructions. He said definitively, "For without me ye can do nothing." (John 15:5) And Paul testifies, "I can do all things through Christ which strengtheneth me" (Phil. 4:13).

This is not a case of God making humans into robots in order to manipulate them for His selfish joy and pleasure. It is, instead, an exercise of their free will. When He created them, in addition to making them in His own image, He also endowed them with the power of choice. Man can choose to disobey Him with the understanding that obedience and disobedience have their individual rewards/consequences (Deut. 30:15–20). Review the paraphrased Anchor Text for Chapter 9.

Number 33: **Genesis 8:22**
While the earth remaineth, seedtime and harvest, and cold and heat,
and summer and winter, and day and night shall not cease.

Paraphrased for Families
(Main Focus: the family in general)

*While human life on earth remains, the vital signs of family relational
health: connection, rapport, bond, and support established in the mind
by God at creation - for them to give the indication of the quality of the
relationships in the active, sound relational mind - shall not cease*

****

Supportive Commentary from *Family Relational
Health - A Biblical, Psycho-social Priority:* Chapter 7

Relational Sensitivity: Nerves and Emotions

The next major issue that this chapter sets out to address is *sensitivity.*
Let us employ a physiological analogy to offer an explanation. Nerves
are to the body as emotions are to the mind (CPH^2). According to
Quora, the brain and the spinal cord process signals from over 60,000
miles of nerves in the network of the body, making us aware of nearly
every impact that the body experiences.

The nervous system uses electrical and chemical means to help
all parts of the body communicate with each other. One cannot help
but remember David's expressed marvel at the complexity of the
human body. "I will praise thee; for I am fearfully and wonderfully
made: marvellous are thy works; and that my soul knoweth right
well" (Ps. 139:14).

Relational sensitivity is far more complex for analytical and
statistical recording than physiological and neurological sensitivity
via the nerves. Given that the subject of relational sensitivity can be
quite broad, we are working in the narrow context of the processing

in the mind of the dynamics and vicissitudes of family relationships. We are keeping focus on the four vital signs of relationship arriving out of the family relational health laboratory that drives this work—connection, rapport, bond, and support—and the emotions these produce that affect the relational mind.

Emotions are so complex that they are more difficult to quantify and measure than nerves, inasmuch as they are real to the quality of behavior and relationships in the mind as nerves are real to the functions of conductivity of the body.

Consider the working definition of Emotion from the Glossary of Book 1, p. 402. *Family Relational Health – A Biblical, Psycho-social Priority.*

Number 34: **1 Corinthians 12:1**
Now concerning spiritual gifts, brethren, I would not have you ignorant.

Paraphrased for Families
(Main Focus: the Family in general)

Now, concerning the brain and the mind with their similarity and difference, family members: I would not want you to be ignorant. They are one and the same, yet mysteriously distinct as God designed their intricate and complementary physiological and psychological functions in the interest of our family relational health, and He will inspire us as we grow in Him, to know them as He is known unto us.

****

Supportive Commentary from *Family Relational Health - A Biblical, Psycho-social Priority* – Chapters 3

Biblical Understanding of the Soul

The apostle says "as thy soul prospereth." Let us establish first of all that there is not an entity or component of the human being that is called the *soul*. At the Creation, God declared that when He blew His breath of life into the clay/earth body He had formed, His breath made the body into a living soul. He did not say that He placed a soul into the man. He said that His breath of life made the man a living soul—implying that before His breath, man was a dead (or preferably a *pre-sin unalive*), not-living soul. (*Dead* was only applicable after sin). God's life-giving breath electrified the not-living soul. It stimulated all the parts—cells, nerves, tissues, glands, organs—and brought them into a functional, living, operational state.

Prior to the creation of man, God did make some living, moving, functional bodies. He simply called them into being, and He did not declare them souls. One stark difference between those living creatures—animals and birds—and the man whom He created is that there was immediate interaction between God and the man.

A *connection* was made and a *rapport* began; they (God and man) began to *bond* as Adam experienced *support* from God. All these have at least one common element: they influence relationships, and therefore our relational heath began with God, hence it is a biblical priority.

When we speak of our spirituality, the root or origin of the concept is from the Bible account of who God is. It says: "God is a Spirit and they that worship Him, must worship Him in Spirit and in truth" (John 4:24). Our spirituality then is the quality and means of our connection and relationship with God.

Going back to the Creation account, when God made man, He built in him a unique capacity to communicate and relate with him, whether they were face to face (Gen. 2:19) or He, God, was in heaven (Gen 22: 17; Deut. 26: 15) and man remained on earth. That means was through the diverse, multifunctional brain–mind combination.

Let us not be confused over the twin word *brain–mind* combination with which God made man. We can read the working definition of the terms *brain* and *mind* in the Glossary of *Family Relational Health A Biblical, Psych-Social Priority* pp. 399 & 408.

Remember: The above is an extract from Chapter 3. To get the clearer, deeper and fullest understanding and application of the text and topic, read the complete chapter in Book 1. *Family Relational Health – A Biblical, Psycho-social Priority.*

Number 35: **1 Corinthians 16:20 and Hebrews 8:11**

Greet ye one another with an holy kiss. And they shall not teach every man his neighbour, and every man his brother, saying, Know the Lord: for all shall know me, from the least to the greatest.

Paraphrased for Families
(Main Focus: the family in general)

As we mature in Christ, no one will need to explain to the other the meaning and boundaries of kissing each other, whether it be in the conjugal relationship between husband and wife or in the social and spiritual relationship between brothers and sisters in the church.

****

Supportive Commentary from *Family Relational Health - A Biblical, Psycho-social Priority*: Chapter 10

The Esteemed Value of Face-to-Face Relationship and Kiss

Seeing that healthy emotional feeling is a part of the love relationship gift from God, it might be little wonder why the memory of that first physical touch beyond the holding of the hands, that kiss, in a healthy relationship between a fledgling husband and wife, is such a cherished memory. That kind of physical and emotional contact, generated from the affective domain of the mind and not merely from the cognitive, is to be highly valued and not taken lightly, as is portrayed in the movie scenes of the entertainment industry.

Inasmuch as lip-kissing between husband and wife in our sinful existence cannot be paralleled with the Holy God breathing in the nostrils of Adam and Eve, the comparative evidence of facial, physical intimacy is the point of reference here. To bring Adam and Eve to life, God initiated a face-to-face relationship by breathing into their nostrils His breath which is life. He could have simply *spoken* it as He did for the animals, but he *did* it!

We have no record to specify how Adam expressed his first physical contact with Eve, but upon seeing her face-to-face, he exulted, "This is now bone of my bone and flesh of my flesh." He did not speak in only spiritual terms but in the physical as well. Since the Fall, face-to-face contact with God had been no longer possible, and one of the desires of human beings is to see God face-to-face again (Gen. 3:6–10, 22–24). Such was the expressed desire of Moses recorded in Exodus 33:16–23.

Despite how we might admire the physique or physical formation of a romantic partner, that physiognomic face-to-face contact is indispensable. The sustained, developmental admiration and approval of the messages from the face generally generate that emotional desire and subsequent magnetic pull to bring the faces together and seal with that sensitive and healthily sensual kiss.

Remember: The above is an extract from Chapter 10. To get the clearer, deeper and fullest understanding and application of the text and topic, read the complete chapter in Book 1. *Family Relational Health – A Biblical, Psycho-social Priority.*

Number 36: **1 Corinthians 16:20 and Hebrews 8:11**
In the mouth of two or three witnesses shall every word be established.

Paraphrased for Families
(Especially for the husbands and wives)

In the eyes of all these witnesses, your love is now publicly established for each other, as is now borne out in the individual expression of your marriage vows. "I now call upon these persons here present to witness ..."

****

Supportive Commentary from *Family Relational Health - A Biblical, Psycho-social Priority:* Chapter 10

The Esteemed Value of Face-to-Face Relationship and Kiss

The value and esteem of that first kiss has been the record in the testimony of thousands of couples (husbands and wives) throughout the centuries of human conjugal relationship. It is even one of the celebrated high points in a Christian marriage ceremony. When the marriage officer pronounces them as "now husband and wife," he tells the husband, "You may now kiss the bride!"

This kiss is usually anticipated and generally greeted with cheers of affirmation from the onlooking family members, friends, and well-wishers. The husband and wife are now sealed and united as one. This does not always imply that they might not have kissed each other before, but "in the mouth of two or three witnesses shall every word be established" (2 Cor. 13:1). Paraphrased is this: "In the eyes of all these witnesses, our love is now publicly established for each other." And this is verily borne out in a section of the marriage vows. "I now call upon these persons here present to witness ..."

This value and esteem about a first kiss was the evident experience of former US First Lady Michelle Obama, as she recorded that cherished memory between her and Barack in her book *Becoming*

Michelle Obama (chapter 9, page 111). "Any worries I'd been harboring about my life and career and even about Barack himself seemed to fall away with that first kiss, replaced by a driving need to know him better, to explore and experience everything about him as fast as I could." A plaque marking the location for their first kiss has been installed on the corner of Dorchester Avenue and Fifty-Third Street in Chicago, USA.

We reaffirm that this intimate and positively healthy emotional act should be engaged in by a man and a woman with the understanding that that level of intimacy is ushering in the one-fleshedness as they begin to recreate themselves, individually, into each other's mind. Correctly understood, this loving act between husbands and wives, although in their sinful, human state, is a miniscule symbolic reflection of when the Holy God of Creation breathed His love and image into the human body and mind, individually; brought them together; and declared that they were not twain, but one.

Furthermore, they understand that the ultimate combined result of their being one—mentally, physically, emotionally, spiritually, and socially—is to be symbolic of the relationship between Christ and His bride-church (Eph. 5:22–32). We need to keep the bar raised on the esteem of the marriage relationship without minimizing any aspect of it: mental, physical, sexual, emotional, spiritual, or social.

Remember: The above is an extract from Chapter 10. To get the clearer, deeper and fullest understanding and application of the text and topic, read the complete chapter in Book 1. *Family Relational Health – A Biblical, Psycho-social Priority.*

Number 37: **Deuteronomy 6:7–9**

And thou shalt teach them diligently unto thy children, and shalt talk of them
when thou sittest in thine house, and when thou walkest by the way, and
when thou liest down, and when thou risest up. And thou shalt bind them
for a sign upon thine hand, and they shall be as frontlets between thine eyes.
And thou shalt write them upon the posts of thy house, and on thy gates.

Paraphrased for Families
(Main Focus: fathers and mothers: The Seven-day Love Plan for Children)

*And these principles of love that I share with you this day shall be fully
understood in your heart, and you shall diligently show them to your child every
seven days of your parent-child relationship. And you shall accept your child,
love your child unconditionally, then go on to discover your child and appreciate
your child. You will then know how to show affection to your child and learn to
praise and commend your child and therefore respect and honor your child.*

****

Supportive **Commentary** from *Family Relational Health - A Biblical, Psycho-social Priority:* Chapter 8

Basic, Primary Facts of the DNRA Theory

In further preparation for study on this important, new perspective
on family relational health, we consider ten facts which are basic to
the understanding of the (BFDBRA) - **BFDNRA**: Some might seem
repetitive but they are really emphatic.

BFDNRA 1: Human existence in its totality is all about relationships.

BFDNRA 2: Relationship is the major experience to be recorded as
the senses become exposed and emotions begin to be produced
in the brain. (Preview Glossary for definition of *emotions* p. 400).

BFDNRA 3: Imperceptive interpretation of emotions begins to
lay the foundation for the perceptions of relationships in the
tender growing years of the child.

BFDNRA 4: From as early as conception, the relational atmosphere
in which the expectant parents, especially the mother live,

can begin to influence the kind of relationship the child could forge and keep as he or she grows into adulthood.

BFDNRA 5: From a normal, healthy conception, a child's brain-mind, in its developmental stages is totally impressionable and is imperceptively recording impressions from his or her mother and the father (if he is present) as well as from other significant persons in whose sphere of influence the mother exists. All this gets to the child via the umbilical connection with the mother.

BFDNRA 6: From birth, the child's *active* and hopefully *sound* relational mind becomes activated as his or her senses begin their lifelong process of collecting and transmitting stimuli and messages to the brain. (See p. 146).

BFDNRA 7: From the time that the child makes that first sound, at birth signaling his or her presence here, she begins the relationship with the new out-of-the-womb environment: "I am here, I am now connected. Henceforth, I will be an integral part of what happens, and I will also influence what happens!"

BFDNRA 8: From birth, the child's mind begins to record impressions of relationship to which he or she is exposed. These impressions are developmental and, if properly and carefully observed, *notifiers* of them will be seen in reactions and responses that the growing baby gives off.

BFDNRA 9: If these *notifiers* are also carefully and properly observed, monitored, and treated, they can give a good indication of the quality of the relationships that the child could grow up to forge and keep.

BFDNRA 10: All relationship vibes (aura) or connections are coded and loaded into the baby's brain-mind, and the decoding of each takes place gradually by associating them with meanings of actions and inactions during the course of development.

Remember: The above is an extract from the Chapter 8. To get the clearer, deeper and fullest understanding and application of the text and topic, read the complete chapter in Book 1. *Family Relational Health – A Biblical, Psycho-social Priority.*

Number 38: **James 3:11–13**

Out of the same mouth proceedeth blessing and cursing. My <u>brethren</u>, these
things ought not so to be. Doth a fountain send forth at the same place
sweet water and bitter? Can the fig tree, my brethren, bear olive berries?
either a vine, figs? so can no fountain both yield salt water and fresh.

Who is a wise man and endued with knowledge among you?
let him shew out of a good conversation his
works with meekness of wisdom.

Paraphrased for Families
(Main Focus: the family in general in the context of the use of social media)

*From the same media (the device) and messenger (you, the person) come texts,
emails, and voice mails with good and bad news?
Do you use your social media to send out encouragement and discouragement at
the same time? How "smart" are you when you use those phones that are called
by the same name and the tablets too, to send out fake news and the Good News,
sensations and speculations, and salvation and inspiration?
Do you consider yourself among those who are wise and reasoning right?
Then make sure that you send out good and healthy communication that
works well with sincerity and genuineness to help in times of need.*

✶✶✶✶✶✶✶✶✶✶✶✶✶✶✶✶

Supportive Commentary from *Family Relational
Health - A Biblical, Psycho-social Priority:* Chapter 6

Unhealthy Mind Directs Unhealthy Body Functions

Paul picks up the lamenting strain from David.

> As it is written, there is none righteous, no, not one:
> There is none that understandeth, there is none that
> seeketh after God. They are all gone out of the way,
> they are together become unprofitable; there is none
> that doeth good, no, not one. Their *throat* is an open
> sepulchre; with their *tongues* they have used deceit;
> the poison of asps is under their *lips*: Whose *mouth*

is full of cursing and bitterness: Their *feet* are swift to shed blood: Destruction and misery are in their ways. (Rom. 3:10–16)

The five body parts identified here are all symbols of the mind and are used to show how various relationships are affected by the mind—employing, as it were, these organs as its agents to demonstrate its true state. The throat, the tongue, the lips, and the mouth are part of the speech mechanism, and the utterance that comes from them is powered by the mind.

The feet represent the mobility aspect of the mind. One means of spreading the natural evil imaginations of the mind is for the body to move from house to house as stated in 1 Tim. 5:13. "And withal they learn to be idle, wandering about from house to house; and not only idle, but tattlers also and busybodies, speaking things which they ought not."

These and other challenges that come from God are not condemnatory; they are not belittling or disparaging. They are intended to create an awareness of the true state of the mind, seeing that we were all born in sin and shapen in iniquity (Ps. 51:5). It is not natural for us to do good from the corrupt and remorseless mind.

Remember: The above is an extract from Chapter 6. To get the clearer, deeper and fullest understanding and application of the text and topic read the complete chapter in Book 1. *Family Relational Health – A Biblical, Psycho-social Priority.*

Number 39: **Romans 10:15**
And how shall they preach, except they be sent? as it is written,
How beautiful are the feet of them that preach the gospel
of peace, and bring glad tidings of good things!

Paraphrased for Families
(Main Focus: the family in general)

And how shall they help in times of crisis, except you are prepared? It is well-known that only those who are conscious and well prepared with healthy minds will be able to conceive good messages and text them with controlled fingers or record them with positive voice, so that the receiver will be blessed with the Good News of peace and hope.

****

Supportive Commentary from *Family Relational Health - A Biblical, Psycho-social Priority:* Chapter 12

Professional Family Relational Treatment

In apportioning the gifts for the administration of the affairs of the Church, which affairs would understandably include ministering to family relational matters, the Holy Spirit gave the gifts of *wisdom* and *knowledge* (1 Corinthians 12:8) In Hebrews 5:14 we are told: "*But strong meat belongeth to them that are of full age, even those who by reason of use have their senses exercised to discern both good and evil.*" '*Full age*' and '*use of their senses*' could be interpreted as alluding to maturity, experience and even competence gained from training and preparation, long practice, peer review and consultation.

This record is reminiscent of the preparation that God gave to Solomon at the beginning of his reign, and in answer to his prayer: "*And God said unto him, Because thou hast asked this thing, and hast not asked for thyself long life; neither hast asked riches for thyself, nor hast asked the life of thine enemies; but hast asked for thyself understanding to discern judgment; Behold, I have done according to thy words: lo, I have given thee a wise and an understanding heart; so that there was none like thee before thee, neither after thee shall any arise like unto thee."* (1 Kings 3:11 & 12)

When all of the above and additional Biblical counsels are put together, we see clearly that God made ample provision, and gave guidance and directives for the effective treatment of the relational challenges that He knew would assail families in the process of time. Implied and understood in these injunctions from the Lord, is the need for proper, professional preparation, given that the issues of life would become more complex and demanding, and the relationships that will be formed, will become equally challenging and potentially exhausting. Undoubtedly, *family relational health, is a biblical psycho-social priority* - God's priority for His children.

Remember: The above is an extract from Chapter 12. To get the clearer, deeper and fullest understanding and application of the text and topic read the complete Chapter 12 in Book 1. *Family Relational Health – A Biblical, Psycho-social Priority.*

Number 40: **2 Peter 3:9**

The Lord is not slack concerning his promise, as some men count slackness; but is longsuffering to us-ward, not willing that any should perish, but that all should come to repentance.

Paraphrased for Families

(Main Focus: husbands and wives)

The God of Families is not trite in His declaration about the sacredness and permanence of marriage as some sinful human beings take it, but He is gracious and patient toward hurting husbands and wives, not wanting them to dissolve their marital bond but that they should come to the correct understanding of its meaning and work toward forgiveness, reconciliation, and restoration of their relationship.

****

Supportive Commentary from *Family Relational Health - A Biblical, Psycho-social Priority*: Chapter 10

Marriage—God's Prerequisite to Procreation

As stated earlier, when God fearfully and wonderfully made the human family (male and female), He had an extensive, all-encompassing role for them to play in the continuation of His Creation plan. One of the major aspects of that role was, and still remains, continuing to make other human beings. As a prerequisite to continue that elevated and esteemed role, they both had to be completely and exclusively committed to each other as a man-husband and woman-wife.

God Himself said it definitively and conclusively at the very beginning. "Therefore shall a man leave his father and his mother, and shall cleave unto his wife: and they shall be one flesh" (Genesis 2:24). Then Jesus reiterated it some four thousand years later as recorded in Matthew 19:4–5 and Mark 10:8. The simple straightforward summary is "And they twain shall be one flesh."

Paul, the apostle to the Gentiles of the New Testament Church, caught the strain, and in the fifth chapter of his letter to the Ephesians, he elaborated on the sacredness and sanctity of the marriage relationship. The Holy Spirit inspired Paul to take it several notches higher by citing the marriage relationship between a husband and wife as a mystery (Eph. 5:22–32). Then he elevates it to the highest possible esteem, that of it being a symbol of the relationship between Christ and the Church. So we see the man and the woman firstly symbolizing and representing the Godhead at their Creation and secondly now symbolizing and representing Christ in the redemption plan.

Remember: The above is an extract from Chapter 10. To get the clearer, deeper and fullest understanding and application of the text and topic, read the complete chapter in *Family Relational Health – A Biblical, Psycho-social Priority.*

Number 41: **Ezekiel 33:1**

Say unto them, As I live, saith the Lord God, I have no pleasure in the death of the wicked; but that the wicked turn from his way and live: turn ye, turn ye from your evil ways; for why will ye die, O house of Israel?

Paraphrased for Families

(Main Focus: husbands and wives)

Counsel and say unto them for me, "As your ever-loving God of Families, I take no delight in seeing your troubled marriage come to an end, but that you both should follow My instructions: change from your hard-hearted way of relating, change from your strong-willed attitude, and get help, for why should you give up on your years of life investment together and lose your marriage, oh married son and daughter of Mine?

****

Supportive Commentary from *Family Relational Health - A Biblical, Psycho-social Priority*: Chapter 10

The Mystery of the Marriage Relationship

This is God who designed the unfathomable mind of the man and the woman. He also conceptualized the marriage bond for them, and it is the omnipresent, omniscient Holy Spirit who keeps their minds together in perfect peace as long as they stay on Him (Isaiah 26:3). With the indwelling, keeping power of the Holy Spirit in his and her heart, the husband and the wife will be empowered to do their part in keeping the mystery alive in their minds.

Keep the mystery of your wife or husband in mind. Do not take him or her for granted. M + M = M. That is to say, marriage plus mystery equals mastery. Both are to strive for the mastery of the relationship and not to master, meaning to subjugate or dominate the other one.

Give respect for the mysterious individuality of his or her being. Always keep your mind open to study and understand the other one. When you do, you will have the bonus experience of the third equation of the marriage mystery: PSS = PMM. As the husband and the wife maintain the study of each other in their family lab, they will happily discover that *progressive spousal study* will result in *progressive marriage mastery.*

Finally, the husband and wife, fearfully and wonderfully made to engage in the mysterious bond of marriage, can go on to live together until death do them part, temporarily. They will reunite at the Second Coming of the Lord Jesus. And, at that mysterious, cataclysmic event, the ultimate symbol of their marriage will be realized, that is the marriage of Christ and His Church (Revelation 19: 7). This was the final mystery about which Paul wrote to the Ephesians.

Remember: The above is an extract from Chapter 10. To get the clearer, deeper and fullest understanding and application of the text and topic read the complete chapter in Book 1. *Family Relational Health – A Biblical, Psycho-social Priority.*

Number 42: **Matthew 5:23**

Therefore if thou bring thy gift to the altar, and there rememberest that thy brother hath ought against thee; Leave there thy gift before the altar, and go thy way; first be reconciled to thy brother, and then come and offer thy gift.

Paraphrased for Families

(Main Focus: the family in general)

So, if in bringing your gifts of praise and glory to Me during your personal, family, or congregational worship, and I (The Holy Spirit) remind you that there was something that went wrong between you and a family member, friend, colleague, or any fellow human, and that the matter is an unresolved issue that you know you need to address, take some time, even to pause in your act of worship that you are engaged in, and genuinely address the issue in your mind, with the intention that with the next opportunity that you get, or that you can create. you will find that person, (if it is not convenient where you are to relate with him or her) and seek to improve that relationship. Rest assured I will wait for you during that pause, and with that healthy state of mind, when you resume, your worship will be even more acceptable to Me than if you had pretended away that unresolved human relationship issue.

****

Supportive Commentary from *Family Relational Health - A Biblical, Psycho-social Priority:* Introduction

Potential Spiritual Disturbance

It would not be surprising if the material contained in this book could even cause some emotional and spiritual disturbances. A good case for such a possibility is the application to the family relational health of Jesus's combined, three-pronged teaching about anger management and interpersonal reconciliation, and making or bringing an offering (worship) to the Lord:

But I say unto you, that whosoever is angry with his brother without a cause shall be in danger of the judgment: and whosoever shall say to his brother, Raca, shall be in danger of the council:

but whosoever shall say, Thou fool, shall be in danger of hell fire. Therefore, if thou bring thy gift to the altar, and there rememberest that thy brother hath ought against thee; Leave there thy gift before the altar and go thy way; first be reconciled to thy brother, and then come and offer thy gift. (Matt. 5:22–24)

His three-point counsel is stark and blunt:

1. Stop where you reach with your offering (worship) upon that all is not well between you and your brother (family member, church member, fellow human being ... whoever).

2. Go back and address the impaired relationship.

3. Then return and continue your offering (worship) to me.

The implied assurance is that the Lord will wait on you when points 1 and 2 take place, because that is the only time when your offering (worship) will be acceptable to Him. The message is profound: Good human relationship is an important part of divine worship. This straightforward, unambiguous approach to working on relationships, and the implication if it is not followed, could indeed be a new dimension to understanding this very arresting parable of the Lord.

The explanation above is not necessarily to be taken in the fullest, literal sense of application. If while one is at worship in the temple, he or she remembers that all is not well between him or her and another person, he or she should stop, leave worship, find the person with whom there is a relational challenge, make it up, and then return to continue worshipping the Lord. Not at all! At the same time, he or she should consciously and conscientiously seek out every possible opportunity to find the other person and make it right after the worship service.

In fact, while there in worship, if the Holy Spirit reminds you of the strained relationship between you and the other person, you can stop or pause in your heart (mind), accept the impressions of the Spirit, and proceed to pray for the other party. You will also make a commitment that at the earliest opportunity, which you can make a deliberate effort to bring forward, you will address the matter with him or her.

Pillar 7: The Protoevangelium and Family Relational Health

When God made the first announcement of the gospel (Genesis 3:15), it was His planned response to heal and restore the broken relationship between the families of heaven and earth,(Gen. 3: 8-10) and the human family members of earth, beginning with the first married couple, Adam and Eve (v.12), and by extension, all subsequent families after them (Rom.3:23). Quality family relational health here on earth is a prerequisite for living with the families of all the ages when Jesus comes for the second time and the earth is made new.

Remember: The above is an extract from the Introduction. To get the clearer, deeper and fullest understanding and application of the text and topic, read the complete Introduction and The 7 Pillars in Book 1. *Family Relational Health – A Biblical, Psycho-social Priority.*

Number 43: **Ephesians 4:30**
And grieve not the Holy Spirit of God, whereby ye
are sealed unto the day of redemption.

Paraphrased for Families
(Main Focus: the family in general)

*Do not resist the impressions that the Holy Spirit makes upon your
mind to improve good family relationship. Such resistance in your
mind can metastasize—grow and spread to affect all aspects of your
relationships with other people—and it becomes more and more difficult
to respond to the feelings and emotional connection with others and
then with God Who alone can heal and save your relationship.*

****

Supportive Commentary from *Family Relational Health - A
Biblical, Psycho-social Priority*: Chapter 10 & Glossary

Conscience

The conscience is like the radar that is designed to keep track of
the movements and to ensure that one stays on course. It gives off a
certain signal if one is veering off the correct path. That signal may
vary in strength, and sometimes come as guilt, remorse, shame or
regret. The conscience is that aspect of the mind planted by God to
help us keep integrity, scruples, principles and morality intact. It is
the GPS or preferably the MPS – Mind Positioning System of our
being.

Mind Position System (MPS): An analogical parallel of the
conscience with the GPS- Global Positioning System. Whereas the
GPS is fed by different satellites/radars, **MPS** is fed by many spiritual,
emotional and social 'radars' – sensitivities, scruples, standards.
norms, etc. which in turn are registered into the conscience for action
to be taken.

The most condemnatory state for one's conscience is for it to be *seared* as mentioned in 2 Timothy 4:2 *"Speaking lies in hypocrisy; having their conscience seared with a hot iron."* A seared conscience is one that is scorched, bone-dry, parched, lacking sensitivity towards right or wrong. In Romans 9: 1, Paul points out that the conscience responds to the impressions of the Holy Spirit and bears witness to His work on the mind: *"I say the truth in Christ; I lie not, my conscience also bearing me witness in the Holy Ghost."*

The Unfathomable Relational Mind

The intricate, complex and mysterious combination and co-ordination of the above four characteristics of the mind, make up the *relational mind*, which David succinctly describes as *marvelous*. (See the differentiation of *Mind* and *Relational Mind* in the Glossary.) It is unfathomable because it is made by The Creator, Who is omnipotent, omniscient, omnipresent and eternal. He simply cannot be explained. This same Creator challenged one of His faithful children, Job: *"Canst thou by searching find out God? canst thou find out the Almighty unto perfection?"* (Job 11:7) The answer is simply and profoundly, No!

It should be understood then, that the part of His creation that is closest to Himself, man, would have been made a close representation of His own unfathomable and incomprehensible nature, so that not even the man can understand himself. Outside of God, and within himself by himself, man can do nothing. (John 15:5) Then Paul reaffirms in Philippians 4:13 that the very opposite is equally true: *"I can do all things through Christ which strengtheneth me."*

Remember: The above is an extract from Chapter 10 and the Glossary. To get the clearer, deeper and fullest understanding and application of the text and topic, read the complete chapter in Book 1. *Family Relational Health – A Biblical, Psycho-social Priority.*

Number 44: **James 4:1**

From whence come wars and fightings among you? Come they not
hence, even of your lusts that war in your members?
Ye lust, and have not: ye kill, and desire to have, and cannot
obtain: ye fight and war, yet ye have not, because ye ask not.

Paraphrased for Families
(Main Focus: the family in general)

*From where do you think that any verbal or physical altercations that you
are experiencing are coming? Couldn't they be coming from the unhealthy
and conflicting desires in your mind? You might be having expectations
that are not possible; you might have threatening causing hurt and damage
that will not get you what you desire; your feuding is not yielding what
you might be hoping to gain. All these failures are because you have not
been asking for them from God, the Right Source of what you need.*

****

Supportive Commentary from *Family Relational Health - A Biblical, Psycho-social Priority*: Chapter 2

Life Struggles and Conflicts

Conflict in a healthy, genuine relationship is not necessarily bad.
Correctly managed, conflict can redound to the benefit of all the
parties concerned in that better understanding can be achieved. As
each party respectfully listens to the view of the other, (not from
an opposing perspective), he or she will exercise openness of mind,
tolerance, and acceptance of another viewpoint.

When it is his or her turn to express an opinion on the issue, it
will be done genuinely, honestly, and truthfully. This contribution
to the discussion is not to counteract or oppose, as is the nature
of government and opposition in parliamentary debates. It seems
sometimes that they just oppose for the mere sake of opposing!

With the two views, positions, or opinions now fully expressed, differing though they may appear, the pace is set for negotiation, compromise, and a genuine effort to come together for the common good. This is summarizing healthy conflict at its best, which should be the experience in all families, and more so in the Christian family.

However, the struggle, and indeed the *wrestling*, that our Anchor Text addresses is not healthy in nature. It is correctly described as not being *ordinary*. That is to say, it does not resemble the above description. It is not regular. This kind of struggle is not borne out of an intent to understand and achieve consensus. It is not normal! In other words, the *wrestling* that is experienced in very troubled relationships that threatens to drive the family members asunder is abnormal.

We need to look deeper and more intently to discover what is motivating them. They are not ordinary! A force outside the parties involved with destructive intention is motivating the wrestling. In the case of marital conflicts, the husband and wife are being pitted against each other without being aware that they are pawns in the hands of a power greater than themselves, and so it is for all other types of family conflicts that are wrestling in nature.

Remember: The above is an extract from Chapter 2. To get the clearer, deeper and fullest understanding and application of the text and topic, read the complete chapter in Book 1. *Family Relational Health – A Biblical, Psycho-social Priority.*

Number 45: **Matthew 23:37**

O Jerusalem, Jerusalem, which killest the prophets, and stonest them that are sent unto thee; how often would I have gathered thy children together, as a hen doth gather her brood under her wings, and ye would not.

Paraphrased for Families
(Main Focus: husbands and wives)

Oh, you hurting husband and wife who are destroying the Marriage contact made between Me and you, you who disparage and turn away counsellors and therapists who are to help you! How often I have wanted to bring your relational minds together as a caring mother animal brings her straying offspring together, but you harden your heart toward each other and consequently lock Me out because you are not willing.

****

Supportive Commentary from *Family Relational Health - A Biblical, Psycho-social Priority*: Chapter 12

Importance of the Family Altar

We must affirm, however, that the Christian family's first response to family relational challenges is earnest, individual, and family prayer. This is to be accompanied with equally earnest searching and study of *God's* words for counsel, guidance, inspiration, and action.

Let us also take caution not to treat God as we normally treat the fire department: we only tend to remember their services at times of crisis. The family altar should always be lit and burning brightly. Family worship should be a daily staple in the menu of their relationship. Then, when any unusual challenge arises, building up the flames of the altar with more intense prayer, even family fasting, would be understood.

In family crisis management, God is always the First Responder; we must first and always take it to the Lord in prayer. In His divine wisdom and as a part of His answer to our prayer, He will direct us to the human support team that He will continue to supervise as they work on His behalf. This is where the paraphrasing of our Anchor Text comes in. "He will, with the relational challenges, also provide His approved human professional way to help, so that you may be able to manage and improve your relationships."

That is why, when the Christian is to see the medical practitioner for any major treatment program, we continue to place it into the hands of the Great Physician, the Balm in Gilead (Jer. 8:22). We go and follow all the instructions and directives of the earthly professional as Jesus implied in Matthew 9:12. "But when Jesus heard that, he said unto them, They that be whole need not a physician, but they that are sick." See also Mark 2:17 and Luke 5:31.

Directly applied in the context of marriage: What more assurance could the Church need that the marital relationship is of top priority of all human relationships to God? Little wonder that it is Satan's primary target. Remember the hurricane – earthquake analogy in Chapter 2: destroy the foundation and the superstructure will crumble to the ground (Review p. 27). The first relationship that the forces of evil attack is marriage. What should be a holy wedlock has become for many couples an unholy deadlock. Marriage in so many people's experiences is a prison, and the wedding ring is the padlock.

Unfortunately, it is clear that for these couples, it was not the hearts and minds that were engaged and bonded together in the marriage. Instead, it was the bodies that were motivated by the populist social acclaim, "They are now married!" There are so many societal ills, stigmas and taboos that assail all the categories of the human family, and the marriage relationship heads the list of those which suffer. Satan and his cohorts are having a field day as he sees this divine institution being trampled under the feet of society, including some segments of the very Church that God has appointed to uphold its dignity and sanctity.

How far-fetched would one consider it to suggest that the innumerable cases of failure of the biblical, fundamental marriage of male to female have given rise (in part) to the various versions of what is considered conjugal love springing up in these days? Some might even reason that if the original form of marriage is failing so miserably, its claim to absoluteness is questionable; therefore, any other model that works should be quite as good and deserves the same respect and status rights. Again we lament: Alas! Satan is having a field day! The Church must rally a godly response.

God Owns the Copyright for Marriage

Deliverance for married couples comes firstly from their understanding that there can be no successful marriage without God being a part of the husband's personal life as equally as He is of the wife's personal life. When He made the man who later became the husband, He, God, established a relationship with him before he (Adam) met his wife. Equally so, when God made Eve, before He brought her to Adam and she became a wife, He established a relationship with her. Adam and Eve knew their Creator, God, before they knew each other.

In premarital counseling, the couple ought to be reminded that an active personal, private premarriage prayer life should not be merged into one active married couple's prayer life. It is critical that each one maintains his and her individual prayer life connection with the Lord, and that itself will strengthen their prayer life as a couple when they meet to light the family altar.

God is the designer of marriage, and He owns the copyright. It is not an institution designed by man. Therefore, its success will be influenced, to a large degree, by the couple's total dependence upon Him for inspiration and guidance. The remainder of the success possibility depends on the combined individual choice of each spouse and their access and use of knowledge and marital relational skills.

Running parallel with the couple's dependence upon God for His inspiration and guidance, and their combined power of choice, is the Church's responsibility to provide adequate, competent, professional strategies for developing marital relational skills. The last bastion of hope for the survival of the family in this age of corruption and moral decadence is the Church. The leadership needs to rise to the occasion and raise the bar of quality relationship by precept and example, so that those within its sphere of influence can receive and give clear and unequivocal evidence that God is still in charge.

For this ideal to be realized, Church leaders need to first live and set the solid, clear example of simply, good Christian married life. In this regard, they should be able to borrow from the apostles and proclaim: "Be ye followers … as I am of Christ" (1 Corinthians 11:1) and "Look on us" (Acts 3:4).

Remember: The above is an extract from Chapter 12. To get the clearer, deeper and fullest understanding and application of the text and topic, read the complete chapter in Book 1. *Family Relational Health – A Biblical, Psycho-social Priority.*

Number 46: **Proverbs 22:28**
Remove not the ancient landmark, which thy fathers have set.

Paraphrased for Families
(Main Focus: the family in general)

Do not erase, tarnish or belittle the foundation landmarks of good,
Bible-based family life that the founding husbands and wives as well as
fathers and mothers have set, following God's ideal from creation.

****

Supportive Commentary from *Family Relational Health - A Biblical, Psycho-social Priority*: Chapter 2

The Family at the Proverbial Crossroads

Ah! We wish victory could be accomplished in a militant and spiritual confrontational shout! It takes much more than that. Some of the families that Satan has succeeded in destroying have been heard to be leading such shouts and singing, "We are marching to Zion!" and "Onward Christian Soldiers, marching unto war." What might have happened to them? Somewhere along the line, they lost focus. Their vigilance, awareness, and watchfulness were compromised, and they became reduced to mere presenters and hearers or the word and not doers (Rom. 2:13; Jas. 1:22).

The ultimate effect of these combined forces is that they have pushed the family to the proverbial crossroads. When one is said to be at a crossroads in life, such a person is in a mental state of confusion, uncertainty, bewilderment, and dilemma. Those are apt descriptions of the family in general today. All the pillars and all the ancient landmarks of good, healthy family relationship are removed or are being removed.

Relativity and conditionality are the new norms of measurement of behavior in every aspect of relationship. The advocacy of the age seems to be saying that there are no expectations or standards that anyone needs to strive toward anymore. Each man (husband, wife, father, mother, child, relative, etc.) sets his or her own standards and moves out to achieve them in this free society without boundaries. Little wonder, therefore, that the family is in an utter state of confusion, uncertainty, bewilderment, and dilemma while at the crossroad, not knowing where to turn.

Remember: The above is an extract from Chapter 2. To get the clearer, deeper and fullest understanding and application of the text and topic, read the complete chapter in Book 1. *Family Relational Health – A Biblical, Psycho-social Priority.*

Number 47: **Psalm 131:3**
Set a guard, O Lord, over my mouth; Keep watch over the door of my lips.

Paraphrased for Families
(Main Focus: the family in general)

*Place a conscious guard over my active, sound mind, oh Lord, and help
me to keep proper watch over its function, because my mouth and my
lips are only the expression mechanism of what my mind produces.*

****

Supportive Commentary from *Family Relational Health - A Biblical, Psycho-social Priority*: Chapter 6

The Tongue: Visible Symbol of the Mind

The Lord used another apostle, James, to speak for Him regarding
the mind and its influence on relationships. This time, James uses
the tongue, that visible section of the speech mechanism. Here are
his detailed findings, loaded with several apt analogies with which
we can fully identify: James 3:1–18.

God has total knowledge of how the mind affects the relational
health of His people. The tongue, which symbolizes speech, which
comes from our thoughts, which are produced in the mind, must be
brought under the full and complete control of the Lord. "The tongue
of the just is as choice silver: the heart of the wicked is little worth"
(Prov. 10:20). "But those things which proceed out of the mouth come
forth from the heart; and they defile the man. For out of the heart
proceed evil thoughts, murders, adulteries, fornications, thefts, false
witness, blasphemies" (Matt. 15:18–19).

The Bible shows that throughout human history, man can only
experience a successful relationship with his God and his fellow men
if he brings his thoughts into captivity to the will of God (2 Cor. 10: 5).
He will then learn to take heed to the counsel of the Lord, his Maker,
as chronicled in God's word.

Unhealthy Mind Directs Unhealthy Body Functions

Paul picks up the lamenting strain from David: "As it is written, there is none righteous, no, not one: There is none that understandeth, there is none that seeketh after God. They are all gone out of the way, they are together become unprofitable; there is none that doeth good, no, not one. Their throat is an open sepulchre; with their tongues they have used deceit; the poison of asps is under their lips: Whose mouth is full of cursing and bitterness: Their feet are swift to shed blood: Destruction and misery are in their ways." (Romans 3:10-16)

The five bodily functions that are identified here are all symbols of the mind and are used to portray how various relationships are affected by the mind, employing, as it were, these organs as its agents to demonstrate its true state. The throat, the tongue, the lips and the mouth are part of the speech mechanism, and the utterance which comes from them is powered by the mind.

The feet represent the mobility aspect of the mind. One means of spreading the natural evil imaginations of the mind is for the body to move from house to house as stated in 1 Timothy 5:13: "*And withal they learn to be idle, wandering about from house to house; and not only idle, but tattlers also and busybodies, speaking things which they ought not.*"

These and other challenges that come from God are not condemnatory; they are not belittling or disparaging. They are intended to create an awareness of the true state of the mind, seeing that we were all *born in sin and shapen in iniquity.* (Psalm 51:5) It is not natural for us to do good from the corrupt and remorseless mind.

Remember: The above is an extract from Chapter 6. To get the clearer, deeper and fullest understanding and application of the text and topic, read the complete chapter in Book 1. *Family Relational Health – A Biblical, Psycho-social Priority.*

Number 48: **Ecclesiastes 6:10–11**
Finally, my brethren, be strong in the Lord and in the power
of His might. Put on the whole armor of God, that you
may be able to stand against the wiles of the devil.

Paraphrased for Families
(Main Focus: the family in general)

In the final end, my brothers and sisters, family members all, be
relationally strong and empowered by the Lord, totally covered by the
family armory of the God of Families, if you are to remain unmoveable
and committed and able to resist the assaults of the last days, that
the devil and his hosts are going to hurl at you and your family.

****

Supportive Commentary from *Family Relational Health - A Biblical, Psycho-social Priority*: Chapter 9

Living Up to God's Standards of Righteousness— His Ten Commandments

Earth therefore became the testing ground for Satan's accusation and the human mind the battlefield, as the forces of evil sought to capture this set of God's intelligent ones to their side. This is a part of the cosmic warfare referred to in Ephesians 6 and paraphrased in chapter 2 of this book, "The Family Under Attack."

The human family is honored by God to be part of the jury, as it were, to vindicate His character, justice, and fair play. This they would do by living in accordance with His loving guidelines of righteousness, which Satan labeled as unfair, and up to which none of God's created beings could truly live. There is a germ of truth in that suggestion, because in our sinful state, we cannot measure up to the standards of God's righteousness. However, God never intended it to be so, because He reminded us that it is "not by might, nor by power, but by my spirit, saith the LORD of hosts" (Zech. 4:6). And

Jesus Himself said, "For without me ye can do nothing." Paul added his human experiential testimony in Philippians 4:13: "I can do all things through Christ which strengtheneth me."

Unfortunately, there are subtle echoes of that accusation continuing even today, when some preachers of the word are suggesting that human beings cannot live up to the expectations of all of God's Ten Commandments, His royal law (Jas. 2:8–12). This is a continuation of Satan's malevolent attack on God, which he began in the Garden of Eden when he suggested to Eve that what God said about the fruit of the Tree of Knowledge of Good and Evil was not true or correct so she could decide to disobey Him (Gen. 3:2–5).

Remember: The above is an extract from the Chapter 9. To get the clearer, deeper and fullest understanding and application of the text and topic, read the complete chapter in Book 1. *Family Relational Health – A Biblical, Psycho-social Priority.*

Number 49: **Philippians 4:6–7**

Be anxious for nothing, but in everything by prayer and supplication with
thanksgiving let your requests be made known to God.
And the peace of God, which surpasses all comprehension,
will guard your hearts and your minds in Christ Jesus.

Paraphrased for Families

(Main Focus: the family in general)

*Be careful not to be engaged in anxious planning and, worse yet, scheming
for the things that your family does not have and will be seemingly difficult
to acquire. Instead, keep constant in prayer, thanking God for what
you have and reaffirming your faith in His providence by mentioning
to Him those that you do not have and need. You will then experience a
peace of mind and satisfaction of heart that you are not able to explain,
which is only possible through the indwelling Spirit of Christ in you.*

****

Supportive Commentary from *The First Aid Kit for Successful Family Life*

Family Togetherness

One sure way to manage the challenges of potential discontentment
in the family, and to be thankful for even the limited resources at
times, is to practice healthy family togetherness. In the publication
mentioned above (a forerunner to *Family Relational Health - A Biblical,
Psycho-social Priority*), eight ways to enjoy family togetherness are
mentioned. Here they are:

1. **Pray Together:** It is still true that: "The Family that prays
   together, stays together." Remember to call each other's name
   in prayer. Remember, you can hold hands, or hug each other
   sometimes as you pray together.

2. **Eat Together:** It does not matter how the work, business or
   study is busy or hectic, God will not countenance all those

efforts, good as they may be - even in the name of His service - if they deprive the family of the opportunity to share together. Meal Time is Prime Time!

3. **Play Together:** Play family games and share healthy jokes together. Loosen up, you husbands and wives; father and mothers; parents and children. Loosen up, all you family members and enjoy each other's company!

4. **Go to Church Together:** That in itself is a testimony of good family living and uniting power of the Gospel. It is understood that various schedules and responsibilities will not make this possible at all times. However, disciplined, mutual efforts and commitment to the counsel of Hebrews 10:25 will make this ideal possible. In the case of families with more than one vehicles, work on using one as is convenient. Do everything in you co-ordinated powers to appear in the house of Lord together.

5. **Sit in Church Together:** Do not allow the 52 weeks to pass and you never Sat Together, Sang Together, Read Together or even learn to Say "Amen" Together!

6. **Share Together:** It is correctly said that sharing is caring. Therefore a sharing family is a caring family. Learn to share the joys and sorrows; the successes and failures; the leisures and responsibilities of home life. One for all and all for one!

7. **Plan Together:** Husbands, do not be satisfied to take all the family decisions by yourselves. Wives, do not always make those major purchases or other plans alone. Consult each other. Parents, let the planning include the children too – depending on the matter at hand. Remember to respect each other's rights and opinions.

8. **Go Out and Socialize Together:** When going on social or recreational events, as much as is humanly possible, do so together. Grow with fondness for each other's company. See each other as a decoration of the other such that the fun indeed, is not seen as being completed, or that it would have been even better were the other family member(s) present.

Remember: The above is an extract from *The First Aid Kit For Successful Family Life.* To get the clearer, deeper and fullest understanding and application of the text and topic, read the complete Kit.

Number 50: **1 Corinthians 4:1–2**

Let a man so account of us, as of the ministers of Christ,
and stewards of the mysteries of God. Moreover it is
required in stewards, that a man be found faithful.

Paraphrased for Families

(Main Focus: the family in general)

*Let family members, beginning with the husband-father, be able to
give an account for the family as representative of the God of Families
and as overseers and managers of the mysterious keeping power of
God. It is understood that such overseers and managers need to have
a high sense of accountability, responsibility, and faithfulness.*

****

Supportive Commentary from *Family Relational Health -
A Biblical, Psycho-social Priority:* Chapter 1 & 11

Invest in Studying Home Labs

A family lab? Is this proposal suggesting that we are to invest
corporate funding in studying how families are to operate? We
should leave fathers and mothers (more so the mothers) to figure
out how to grow, discipline, and bring up the children while the big
brains—the scholars, scientists, technologists, and experts (who do
not seem to be products of those homes!)—address the larger issues
of the development and advances of society.

Since long before the 2020 outbreak of the global pandemic of
COVID-19, and even before the 1918 Spanish flu pandemic (and
others of the kind), the pandemic of bad human and family relational
health has been known and growing exponentially. Maybe, much
to our international failure, there has been no WHO, or preferably,
no FWHO (Family World Health Organization), to galvanize world
family consensus and arrest the matter of the decadence of human
relationship and behavior. We know for sure that this viral human

relationship plague did not begin in Wuhan, Hubei Province, China, but in virtually every hamlet, village, community, town, city, and indeed every country in the world.

By raising the bar and seeing the family as the basic, fundamental lab unit of society, we will better understand the complex dynamics of its inner working and of family relational health. We will be better able to produce the quality of life about which we can only dream amid the thundering triumphs of the scientific, industrial, technological, and other laboratories of this twenty-first century.

God Designed Sex/Gender Harmony

We reaffirm that in God's original plan, Eve was not made subject to Adam's dominion as were the animals made to him first and by extension to her equally. She was equally human as Adam, both being made to complementarily represent the image of God. Complementary as used here suggests that they were intrinsically not identical but compatible to represent and fulfil different aspects of the image of God.

Eve was to identify with Adam's leadership, and Adam was to respect and incorporate her into the operations (work and worship) of the home and family that they would build together, under his God-appointed leadership. Was that pattern of operation to have been continued towards and until Eden is restored?

The Bible is replete from Genesis to Revelation with the ideal alluded to and implied above, despite the impact of sin, and it is all ours for the full understanding even in this age of the sex-gender controversy, as we individually and together, men and women, males and females seek the guidance of the indwelling Holy Spirit. The pre-eminence in terms of order and timing (not the same as predominance) of the male outside of his God-given positive responsibility, accountability, and answerability for the well-being of his family, cannot and should not be tolerated.

Family relational health will never be experienced if this scourge is not eradicated and healed. The husband is the head of the wife, as he, the man, submits to the headship of Christ (Eph. 5:22–23), Who has the well-being of both of them at His heart. As long as He is in charge of them, all should be well.

Remember: The above is an extract from Chapters 1 & 11. To get the clearer, deeper and fullest understanding and application of the text and topic read the complete Chapters 1 & 11 in Book 1. *Family Relational Health – A Biblical, Psycho-social Priority.*

Number 51: **Romans 12:16**

Be of the same mind one toward another. mind not high things, but condescend to men of low estate. Be not wise in your own conceits.

Paraphrased for Families

(Main Focus: the family in general)

Strive to be of the same healthy mind in thinking about each other. Do not concentrate on attaining loftiness in status and material things, but even with such attainments, be humble and relate genuinely with people who are of simple and low status in life. Do not be foolish to think of yourself as being better than other people.

****

Supportive Commentary from *Family Relational Health - A Biblical, Psycho-social Priority*: Chapter 8

Relationship Fact 9:
Healthy human relationship is not natural.

Forging and keeping a healthy relationship to benefit all the persons involved does not come naturally and easily for everyone in the same way. David states the reason: he (as well as all of us) "… was shapen in iniquity; and in sin did my mother conceive me" (Ps. 51:5). Self-serving or selfishness is the natural state of the unregenerate, sinful relational mind.

The naturally selfish mind is borne out of self-preservation—the first law of nature. *Farlex Idioms and Slangs Dictionary International* suggests that "Every living thing will fight to survive; it is natural to think of yourself first. When Joe's best friend was arrested, Joe pretended not to know him. *Perhaps it wasn't very loyal of me*, he thought." This was exactly the relational predicament in which Peter found himself, at the arrest of his Friend and Master, Jesus. He denied knowing Him in the interest of protecting himself from being accused and treated the same way (Mark 14:66–72).

God's counsel through the apostle Paul to the Philippians is the very opposite: "Let nothing be done through strife or vain glory; but in lowliness of mind let each esteem other better than themselves. Look not every man on his own things, but every man also on the things of others" (Phil. 2:3–4). That is the new law for healthy relationship: selflessness in reference to the well-being of the other person in the relationship. (See how Moses refigured Jesus - Exodus 32: 32; John 15: 13; Romans 5: 8 in the principle of selflessness).

Applied, this means that in the case of marriage, ideally, the husband's focus is not to be on how much his wife is going to love and care for him, but how much he is going to love and take care for his wife. The converse is equally true: ideally, the wife's focus is not to be on how much her husband is going to love and care for her, but how much she is going to love and take care of her husband. Here, both will be engaged in a kind of healthy and even holy competition, albeit unannounced. And the principle would ideally go across every aspect of human relationship. Selflessness is the ultimate test of love.

This ideal is not natural and is well-nigh impossible, save for the continuous indwelling power of the Holy Spirit in the heart and mind of each individual in the relationship. "Let this mind be in you, which was also in Christ Jesus" (Phil. 2:5).

Remember: The above is an extract from Chapter 8. To get the clearer, deeper and fullest understanding and application of the text and topic, read the complete chapters in Book 1. *Family Relational Health – A Biblical, Psycho-social Priority.*

Number 52: **Isaiah 1:18**

Come now, and let us reason together, saith the LORD: though
your sins be as scarlet, they shall be as white as snow; though
they be red like crimson, they shall be as wool.

Paraphrased for Families

(especially for family in general)

*Get together and reason out your relational challenges, the Lord counsel
family members. Although some issues might appear confused in pixelated
red and orange, they can be made crystal clear; some might be more negative
with a deeper red and purple appearance, but they too can be resolved and
your relational minds made clear, light, and healthy as valued sheep wool.*

****

Supportive Commentary from *Family Relational Health - A Biblical, Psycho-social Priority*: Chapter 6

Healthy Hate in the Relational Mind

As family members, we are to hate every thought and act of evil,
whether we are doers or observers. This must have been God's
mindset when He inspired eighty-seven references to *hate* as recorded
in the King James Version of the Bible. He expressed protest against
those relational evils. Here He speaks through Solomon:

> These six things doth the Lord hate: yea, seven are an
> abomination unto him: A proud look, a lying tongue,
> and hands that shed innocent blood, An heart that
> deviseth wicked imaginations, feet that be swift in
> running to mischief, A false witness that speaketh
> lies, and he that soweth discord among brethren."
> (Prov. 6:12–19, emphasis on verses 16–19)

Then, through Zechariah, He offers heavenly psychotherapy to
heal those malevolent, immoral, malicious, and criminal acts.

> These are the things that ye shall do; Speak ye every
> man the truth to his neighbor; execute the judgment
> of truth and peace in your gates: And let none of you
> imagine evil in your hearts against his neighbor; and
> love no false oath: for all these are things that I hate,
> saith the Lord. (Zech. 8:16–17)

In looking at marriage, His foundation plan for human relationship, He healthily used the same word *hate* to express His indignation against those who distort it or make light of it, resulting in a divorce.

> Yet ye say, Wherefore? Because the Lord hath been
> witness between thee and the wife of thy youth,
> against whom thou hast dealt treacherously: yet is she
> thy companion, and the wife of thy covenant. And did
> not he make one? Yet had he the residue of the spirit.
> And wherefore one? That he might seek a godly seed.
> Therefore, take heed to your spirit, and let none deal
> treacherously against the wife of his youth. For the
> Lord, the God of Israel, saith that he hateth putting
> away: for one covereth violence with his garment,
> saith the Lord of hosts: therefore, take heed to your
> spirit, that ye deal not treacherously. (Mal. 2:14–16)

In an effort to destroy those forces that will incite, instigate, or engage in unhealthy relationships among His people, God provides a replacement therapy to stabilize and strengthen those relational minds. Through His inspired word, He shows the positive state of mind that will influence quality, steadfast relationships to be experienced firstly in the home, the Church, and then in society. He speaks through James.

> If any of you lack wisdom, let him ask of God, that
> giveth to all men liberally, and upbraideth not; and it

shall be given him. But let him ask in faith, nothing wavering. For he that wavereth is like a wave of the sea driven with the wind and tossed. For let not that man think that he shall receive any thing of the Lord. A double minded man is unstable in all his way.

Here we see God alluding to the issue of ignorance that can have untold negative effects on family relationships.

Remember: The above is an extract from the Chapter 6. To get the clearer, deeper and fullest understanding and application of the text and topic read the complete chapters in Book 1. Family Relational Health – A Biblical, Psycho-social Priority.

Section 4

Appendices

Appendix 1

The Twelve-Point Private, Personal Prayer Plan

Introduction

In the Christian life, Jesus is correctly referred to as our Example, and unquestionably, He is. He said it in many ways such as "If any man serve me, let him follow me; and where I am, there shall also my servant be: if any man serve me, him will my Father honour" (John 12:26). And Peter echoed it as he counseled, "For even hereunto were ye called: because Christ also suffered for us, leaving us an example, that ye should follow his steps."

The exhortation to follow Christ in every aspect of our lives is always held out to us as the preferred, ideal way to order our daily pattern of living. All of His good deeds of kindness and compassion, His words of peace and assurance, and His teachings and sermons of inspiration and hope are the standards by which we are to live in thought, words, and deeds.

It appears, however, that one of Jesus's fundamental and most exemplary practices has evaded much of our attention. Apart from the Sermon on the Mount (Matthew 5, otherwise referred to as the Beatitudes), one of the most quoted and celebrated teachings of the Savior that is used in the Christian world is the Lord's Prayer (Matthew 6:11–13). Outside of church services, the Lord's Prayer is repeated during devotional exercise in many schools—still, thank God! Even in some corporate companies, especially those that are owned and managed by Christians, the revered and hallowed prayer is said.

Unfortunately, we do not seem pay equal attention to the Lord's pattern of prayer or His Private, Personal Prayer lifestyle. Why is that aspect of His example not being taught and emphasized with fervor equal to His teachings and deeds? In the following twelve steps, effort is made to amplify some practical lessons that can be learned from practicing Jesus's early morning and late evening prayer lifestyle.

If Jesus, who Himself was, is, and has always been God, but in His human form, saw it necessary to have those Private, Personal early morning time with the Father, isn't that an example that we should be following in our Christian life as we strive to be like Christ?

Prerequisites for Developing a Private, Personal Prayer Life Like Jesus

Introspection. Read the characteristic of the maturing, relationally healthy Christian in Number 1 of the paraphrased Bible verses. Do some earnest introspection and ask yourself if those descriptions are true of you. If you are not sure, or if you want to be certain that they are, then, with an open mind, go on to read the very opposite descriptions of the failing, relationally unhealthy Christian outlined on Number 2. Be true to yourself as to which one fits you.

If honestly within yourself, Number 1 is not in sync with what you know about yourself, then it could be difficult for you to develop and maintain the Private, Personal Prayer lifestyle. Why? Because one of the positive, attitudinal states of mind for such a lifestyle is humility anchored in sincerity of the mind. That humility will help you to fall prostrate before God in body (preferably kneeling or bowing) and in mind, (consciously and conscientiously). In adopting such a posture in body and mind, it automatically helps to remove any sense of self-importance and increases the sense of dependence upon and before the One on Whom you call.

Humility and contrition. One spiritual challenge against developing and maintaining a Private, Personal Prayer life is the fact that such setting cannot be done in a proud and conceited state of mind. In the act of Private, Personal Prayer, the only human being who can hear what you say is yourself.

To listen to oneself confessing and admitting to sins, faults, weaknesses, and all flaws of character is simply not easy. It is verily true that it is hard to be humble! And no guilty verdict can be more painful to accept than that pronounced by one's own living conscience. (See the meaning of Conscience – the MPS – Mind Positioning System – in the Glossary of *Family Relational Health, A Biblical, Psycho-social Priority*)

Some important questions that come here are these: What happens to me when I hear what I pray? What effects do my prayers have on me? Maybe some persons just cannot take the disciplining that a stirred conscience (illuminated by the Holy Spirit) will attempt to put them through. In order to avoid that, they do not engage in the kind of earnest, Private, Personal Prayer that is being advocated here.

Let us take a closer look at the conscience. The conscience is like the radar that is designed to keep track of movements and to ensure that one stays on course. It gives off a certain signal if one is veering off the correct path. That signal may vary in intensity and can at times come as guilt, remorse, shame, regret, and contrition. The conscience is that aspect of the mind planted by God to help us keep integrity, scruples, principles, and morality intact.

The most condemnatory state for one's conscience is for it to be *seared*, as mentioned in 2 Timothy 4:2. "Speaking lies in hypocrisy; having their conscience seared with a hot iron." A seared conscience is one that is scorched, bone-dry, parched, and lacking sensitivity toward right or wrong. In Romans 9:1, Paul points out that the conscience responds to the impressions of the Holy Spirit and bears witness to His work on the mind. "I say the truth in Christ; I lie not, my conscience also bearing me witness in the Holy Ghost."

The Narcissist and Private Personal Prayer

The person who will suffer most from the experience of a stirring, soul-searching prayer is one who has narcissistic traits or is a full-blown narcissist. The last state of mind for this person is to accept being told that he or she is wrong, or that there is a weakness in what he or she does.

It can be difficult for the narcissist to be told that he or she is ignorant or that there is a shortfall in his or her knowledge and ability. Read more details about this type of person in chapter 4 of *Family Relational Health - A Biblical, Psycho-social Priority.* The Private, Personal Prayer Plan puts one into a 'publican' state of mind (Luke 18:9–14), and the first characteristic of that state of mind is humility.

It is noteworthy that a narcissistic person can do well in a public prayer. How so? Because in most cases, such prayer would be pharisaical, as exemplified by the Pharisee in the case Jesus cited in Luke 18. Such public prayer can be expressed eloquently and passionately because he or she has an audience who will be impressed by the manifested fervency and even agony of heart. Unlike the Pharisee's, the public prayer does not always have to be personal. It can be movingly and persuasively expressed on behalf of the congregation and any specific matter that he or she might have been asked to pray about.

Some narcissists can be excellent players who know all too well how to commandeer and even manipulate the emotions of the listeners even during the act of prayer. Unfortunately, when such a person goes into that quiet place where he or she is to reflect and reckon with how he or she did in the recently ended service, instead of a sense of recrimination and repentance for the hypocritical showing, there is reveling in the acclamation expressed by the congregation. A Private, Personal Prayer life could be nothing more than a ritual for such person.

There is hardly any sense of penitence and emptying of self; that sense of unworthiness and nothingness and the need for an infilling by the Spirit of Christ is just not there. On the other hand, regardless of his or her status in life, an individual who, by the indwelling Spirit of the Lord, maintains a humble, contrite mind will always find it natural to develop and maintain a Private, Personal Prayer life patterned off that exemplary one of Jesus Christ.

When a person lives in a sustained Private, Personal Prayer life, it will be reflected on the quality of his or her lifestyle and interpersonal relationships. There is a transforming effect on what exudes from him or her, coming out of the closet as mentioned by Jesus in Matthew 6:6. In that closet experience, emptiness of self and selfishness take place and a replacement therapy of simplicity, modesty in speech, and meekness in demeanor is performed by the Holy Spirit.

There are no boastful, loud and ostentatious utterances such as:

"I am a Praying Person."
"I am a Prayer Warrior."
"When I Pray, the heaven moves."
"Satan can't stand around me, because my Prayer will drive him to hell."

There is no where in Jesus' life that such haughtiness of spirit was displayed. Nor was it seen in the lives of any of the apostles. Spiritual fervency, ardour and passion are expressed in simplicity, resonant composure with joy and fervour, attributing all to the quite but deep working of the Holy Spirit. This manifestation arrests and attracts the listeners to a desire for such an experience, instead of making them feel that they can never attain that level of the 'praying giant' who mesmerises them with his or her great spiritual attainment.

We ought to be very careful of setting up expected standards of behavior and utterances by persons based on their prayer life. It remains true, however, that humility, sincerity, sweetness, and genuineness will be the hallmark of such person's character. Those qualities of Christ will naturally exude from the person who follows Jesus's Private, Personal Prayer.

Let us now review some of the references to Jesus's Private, Personal Prayer life, not only in the early mornings but at other times of the day. Then against the lessons from those, let us consider the twelve points below on how we can set out, by His grace, to establish (if we are not yet doing so), the early morning, Private, Personal Prayer Plan as the Holy Spirit will inspire and direct us.

Jesus's Private Personal Prayer Life

1. Mark 1:35
"Very early in the morning, while it was still dark, Jesus got up, left the house and went off to a solitary place, where he prayed."

2. Matthew 14:23
"After he had dismissed them, he went up on a mountainside by himself to pray. When evening came, he was there alone."

3. Luke 6:12
"One of those days Jesus went out to a mountainside to pray, and spent the night praying to God."

Preamble to the Pointers

The action steps below are intended to be practiced in as ideal a setting as described. One's personal setting (where you live) might not make it always possible to follow every step, every time as outlined here. Do not be discouraged. Do the best you can, and God will honor your sincerity and bless your efforts.

We consider the Prayer Points so potent, we will use the symbolic code P^4 (P to the 4th power) P^4- **Point 1:** signaling that in this Prayer Plan, the Three Members of the Godhead (Father, Son and Holy Spirit) are joined with the **1 Praying human being**, and therefore confirming that when the Divine is joined with the human, the power is invincible.

P^4 Point 1: Challenge Yourself to Follow Jesus' Example

Practice Jesus's example. He got up in the early morning, before the break of day, and prayed to His Father in heaven.

Remember

If for any reason early morning is not possible, an evening option is given. Select the most convenient time, offer it to the Lord, and He will work with you.

P^4 Point 2: Build and Maintain Your Desire

Have a genuine, passionate, longing desire to talk with and hear from the Lord via the impressions of the Holy Spirit upon your heart / mind.

Remember

"And ye shall seek me, and find me, when ye shall search for me with all your heart" (Jeremiah 29:13).

P⁴ Point 3: Disciplined Training

Discipline yourself to get up early at your best, comfortable, and even *sacrificial* time.

<u>Remember</u>

It takes a disciplined effort to grow and mature as a Christian. "Gather my saints together unto me; those that have made a covenant with me by <u>sacrifice</u>" (Psalm 50:5). This could mean "sacrificing" or giving up the time when some more sleep would be welcomed!

P⁴ Point 4: Manage Light Distraction

When you awake in the early morning, do not turn on all of the lights or, as much as it is possible and lies within your power, avoid the fully lit place as that can lead to even a small distraction, which you do not want to happen. Maybe a peripheral light (small, dim light) can be preferred to a central one in the area in which you are going to meet with the Lord.

<u>Remember</u>

Keep the atmosphere around you quiet, calm, and serene.

P⁴ Point 5: Manage Movement Distraction

Before you sit in quietness, go to the bathroom, if you must, so as to avoid any urge to break your concentration when you begin to meditate and pray.

<u>Remember</u>

This time is like a mini-fasting that is devoted only for prayer, so as much as is humanly possible, you do not want to get engaged into any other regular activity.

P⁴ Point 6: Preferred Praying Posture

Kneeling is the preferred praying posture of contrition and humility before God, but if you have to remain seated or even standing, given different possible circumstances, do so telling yourself, "I am in direct contact with God right now!"

<u>Remember</u>

If you want to sit first and repeat your favorite assurance from the Lord (meaning your favorite Bible verse), quietly sing or preferably hum a hymn. Feel free to do so. The important idea now is to savor the calmness and quietness of the time and gather your spiritual bearing, then slowly fall on your knees before the Lord.

P⁴ Point 7: Fix Your Focus

As you kneel, fix your mind and thoughts upon the Lord. Try to conceptualize or visualize God up in heaven; imagine Jesus talking with you personally. Do not worry if your mind wanders at times. God understands and will give you the victory in the process of time with disciplined, consistent practice.

<u>Remember</u>

Be conscious, conscientious, and consistent. This is a sure way that you will grow spiritually in the Lord.

P⁴ Point 8: Sense the Presence of God

Remain quiet and allow your mind to have that living, live connection with God. Sense the hovering of the Holy Spirit transporting you by faith into the presence of God in heaven. Sense the aura and holiness of the place as Jacob did. "Truly, the Lord is in this place" (Genesis 28:16).

Remember

Wherever you are, God is, and all will be well.

Remember too

> "When every other voice is hushed and in quietness
> we wait before Him, the silence of the soul makes
> more distinct the voice of God" (*Desire of Ages*, p. 363).

P⁴ Point 9: Listen to, and be Inspired by Your Prayer

Speak/pray gently and audibly enough for your own hearing. There is a psycho-spiritual impact of *"when I hear what I pray"* as the Spirit Himself will inspire some of the very utterances that you make. They can in turn impress you as you hear the very expressions from your own mind.

You do not always need to pray out aloud. You can concentrate your thoughts directly to the Lord. A combination of verbal or spoken as well as silent/whispered thought expressions (and groaning that you do not want to utter) is quite fine. Whichever way you choose, you are in communication with the Lord. (See Roman 8:26)

Special Note

You do not have to worry about Satan hearing and intercepting your prayer when you pray audibly. That has been a battle for saints down through the ages as in the case of Daniel. (See Daniel 10:11–13.) Keep on praying. God will hear and answer you, because the gates of hell cannot and will never prevail against you and God (Matthew 16:8). And Michael, Himself will intervene against such forces as He did for Daniel (Daniel 10: 10-14)

Remember

> "Prayer is the opening of the heart to God as to a
> friend" *(Steps to Christ*, p. 93). "Be still and know that
> I am God" (Psalm 46:10).

P⁴ Point 10: Practice the Key Components of Prayers

Express your prayers in *thanksgiving, praise, confession,* and
supplication to God.

Tell Him exactly how you feel. State it as *you* want to. Only He is
hearing what you feel impressed to say to Him.

Remember

Of all the billions of His children on earth, you are now *alone*
with God. Use the time to be fully and totally personal with Him.

Special Reminder

Feel free to use expressions with which you are comfortable. You
do not have to address God as "Thee" and "Thou." Be assured that
God accepts "You" and "Your" when you simply and sincerely address
Him. You can even repeat scriptural promises and claim them from
Him. He is all yours now!

P⁴ Point 11: Rise with Assurance and Confidence

Spend quality time with the Lord. Rise from your knees confidently.
When you open your eyes, you should sense that feeling of returning
and reconnecting to earth, because you were transported by the Spirit
to the very throne room of God. You should rise in an *expectant mode
of mind,* believing that God heard your prayer and will, in His good
time and manner, answer you.

<u>Remember</u>

Be patient with yourself as you wait upon the Lord for His answers.

P⁴ Point 12: Maintain the Anticipated Return

Look forward to the next morning (or time) when you will have that rich, high spiritual experience with the Lord. Be consistent, and watch your spiritual life mature.

<u>Remember</u>

Testify to others and encourage them to follow this Private, Personal Prayer Plan. That will strengthen your conviction and faith and your relationship with God.

Appendix 2

Twelve Tips for Growing and Stabilizing
The Christian Marriage

Introduction

There is virtually an endless supply of guidelines, instructions, suggestions, counsels, advice, and recommendations that are available to help married couples (husbands and wives) to experience a long-lasting and mutually fulfilling marriage. Marital ignorance should not be an excuse for failures in this enlightened age. Alas, it is still so!

The suggestions below, written to be as simplified and applicable as possible, are presented on the assumption that the Reader subscribes to and desires to uphold the ideals of the Christian principles of marriage, as taught in the Holy Bible, 'God's Family Book'.

Each married couple is encouraged to consider doing them if they are not presently doing so, and for those who are, continue to reaffirm and do them. Premarital couples (fiancé and fiancée) are also encouraged to embrace the suggestions and commit their minds to practicing them from the very day that they get married. In the effort to maintain the progressive and developmental impact on the mind of the couple as they read, we will refer to each Tip as a **Marriage Growth and Stabilizing Recommendation (MGSR)**.

MSGR 1: Develop and Maintain a Daily, Private Personal Prayer Life.

It is best done early in the morning, following Jesus's pattern recorded in Mark 1:35. Alone with God. This takes self-discipline, but it works and is worth the effort, and maybe even considered as being indispensable for your Personal Spiritual Growth. (See Appendix 1: *The Twelve-Point Private Personal Prayer Plan*).

MSGR 2: Talk Directly With God Every Day.

Call each other's name to Him and ask for mutual strength and love. This spiritual exercise deepens your love and commitment for each other when you, as an individual, make a conscious, private effort to mention your spouse by name in prayer. When you do, every now and then, find the opportunity to tell your spouse, "I prayed for you. I lifted you up to the Lord!" It can be an added assurance that you are your spouse's Spiritual Prayer Partner.

MSGR 3: Be Sure To Pray Together Every Day.

Kneel together, hug and pray together, and hold hands and pray together. Whichever way, just pray together and love and be blessed together.

MSGR 4: Be Sincere, Sweet Friends Together.

Play together, and share little fun together! Laugh and joke and kiss together. Remember that little 'funny' or special name that you call him or her that only the two of you know? Use it up! It helps to keep you childlike, simple, and sweet together!

Cherish your intimate life experience together. Remember that intimacy is not limited to your sexual experiences. You should be intimate mentally, emotionally, spiritually, socially, and definitely physically. With specific reference to physical and sexual intimacy, you should be able to share such moments unconditionally, unreservedly, and uninhibitedly and be vulnerable with each other.

Your sexual life should be mutually satisfying and be a part of your growing together. Your sexual experiences should ideally be spontaneous. Always keep the welcoming surprise element even to have him or her wondering what he or she will come up with next!

Remember, your bodies and minds 'belong' to each other. None should be a servant to meet the other one's sexual desires and needs. Work lovingly for each other's sexual satisfaction. As in any other major aspects of your marital experience, your sexual health takes time and patience, knowledge and skills to be developed.

Anchor your rich, sexual experience on sound biblical passages, such as 1 Corinthians 7:3–5 and Hebrews 13:4. It is also understood that the relationally expressive book of Songs of Solomon cannot be left out, especially as we allow the Holy Spirit to lead us to understand the double interpretation and application of its message. It elevates the symbolism of the intimate relationship between a husband and wife to point out the intimate work and relationship of the Spirit in our lives, culminating in the relationship between Christ and the Church.

Strive for the esteemed level of the understanding of being "Friends" as Jesus raised the relationship between the disciples and Himself. He elevated it from "servants" to "Friends" (John 15:15). See yourselves as not serving each other as partners but relating with each other as "friends" of the highest possible order.

MSGR 5: Be Simply Honest And Open With Each Other.

Avoid suspicion. Do not deceive each other. If you did something that he or she did not know about but which would have caused hurt, firstly ensure that it is totally and completely ended. Be sure that you cease and desist. Accept God's invitation to come to Him and address the matter. Be earnest and sincere with God and agonize with Him about it in your Private, Personal Prayer time. (See P4 Point 9 in Appendix 1)

Thank Him for protecting or shielding you both from the exposure of your wrong, which could have had devastating effects on your relationship. Remember that it is not every spiritual challenge that affects your salvation together. Some are for you personally and are best dealt with between you alone and Your God together!

Once you are genuine and sincere about it, His assurance of forgiveness, cleansing, and restoration will be given to you. Accept His forgiveness by faith, rejoice in your heart, and let that free, forgiven spirit shine out in your natural attitude and behavior toward your spouse.

Make sure that there are no negative residual effects on you that will in any way affect him or her or give, or imply cause for concern. Be careful not to allow any residual guilty state of mind to influence the relational atmosphere that you create between you and your spouse. Pray for strength to live and enjoy the forgiven life. Do not speak and behave with guilt. Such behaviour can raise unnecessary concern or even suspicion in your spouse and affect the relationship.

To Tell or Not to Tell? When You Are The Offending One

Where the situation could and will likely become known to, or be discovered by your spouse, follow the suggestions above regarding your agonizing private prayer with the Lord, seeking His forgiveness and strength.

Ideally, it is best for you to create a comfortable atmosphere in which to tell the matter to him or her. Be prepared for the possible human element of surprise and other possible, even negative emotions or reactions. Keep your calm and composure, and silently call on the Lord to honor your sincerity. Respond in a genuine and composed manner to comments or questions from him or her.

Do not demand understanding and acceptance from him or her. Avoid statements such as: "Get over it. It is in the past now." "Can't you just let go and understand?" Be your genuine, natural repentant self and offer the occasional little statements of assurance and understanding of your awareness of how the situation might impact him or her. Let him or her see and feel your genuine, sincere heart as you speak. Offer him or her time to process the matter if he or she expresses that desire. Express your willingness to continue talking through and working the issue or challenge to a good, mutually enriching, and stabilized marriage.

Express sincere thankfulness to him or her for being there with and for you, and reaffirm your commitment and love for him or her. Offer to pray together, and do so as amicably as indicated by him or her. All this could require a lot of patience and composure on your part. Always keep the prayer in your heart for God's divine intervention.

Avoid any temptation to be reactive and defensive. You may offer explanations where it is necessary to do so, but do not defend yourself in any aspect of your wrong. Remember to be patient with him or her. Do not expect a 'light flick-switch,' instantaneous response such as "Let us now forget it and move on!"

The human relational mind does not necessarily work that fast; it has to process some matters, depending on the nature, intensity, and magnitude. Avoid making comparison between you and him or her as to how you might have handled any matters of this or similar nature in the past, if there were such instances.

When You Are the Offended One

Where you are the spouse at the receiving end, that is, the one who is offended, keep a prayer in your heart. Practice sincerity and openness of heart and mind. Be composed and respond to your spouse in accordance with the sincerity and honesty that he or she exudes. Be your genuine self as the Spirit impresses you to be at this potentially sensitive time. Feel and accept the humanity of your spouse. This is a good testing time to remember where the Lord's Prayer says "and forgive us of our debts as we forgive our debtors" (Matthew 6:11–13).

Do not crush his or her demonstrated sense of penitence and humility. Where those are shown clearly by him or her, accept and even affirm them. This counsel is called *forgiveness!* This is not forcing you into fast-forward, and to desensitize your human and spousal feeling of hurt, disappointment, or even betrayal of trust. Those are to be respected and even expected. It is understood that you could experience those and other negative emotions.

While not making light of such possible realities above, the counsel is discouraging you from making unnecessary rewinding, repeating, and questioning. This is not asking you to shelve your feeling or need to ask for any clarity, but avoid making such enquiries for mere curiosity, or with any intent to deepen his or her sense of remorse and guilt.

The earlier, and as quickly as you can respond healthily and help to bring about calm and composure to the situation, the better it could be for both of you. Where you can take the upper, Christlike posture at this time, the better it will be for your spiritual growth and development, and it will redound to the mutual benefit of you both.

Follow these and any other guidelines that the Spirit might impress upon you. If the matter is beyond your ability to mutually resolve, seek professional help individually and together.

MSGR 6: Practice the Principle of Daily Reunion.

a. When you awake in the morning, greet each other with mutual thankfulness to God that you are reunited, coming out of sleep and darkness into light and 'life' again! See the hymn "New every morning is the love" by John Keeble (1822). Note the expressed sentiments in stanza 1 about being: "restored to life and pow'r and thought."

b. Keep the same practice when you return home each day or time that you go apart out of the house. Enjoy the opportunity to be back together. Give God thanks. Share with each other some of the experiences you might have had while being apart. Be open and encouraging.

c. Each time that you are parting, including going to sleep, do so with a wishful cheer, such as "See you later," "Be safe," "Love you," "Good night. Sleep well," or "Keep in touch."

While you are away from the home, make genuine effort to keep in touch with each other. An occasional little "checking up on you" should be healthy and welcomed, even to paving the way for the reunion later and—who knows?—even with a promise of "good things" to come! (See Songs Numbers 49 and 51.)

This little "checking up on you," done with good, moderate timing apart, should not be viewed with tension and suspicion and a sense of being kept under surveillance such as: "Why are you calling me (so often)?" "Why are you checking on me!?"; "Are you watching me?" It should be valued and done and received as evidence of caring love and with the best intent of heart.

Private Communication Abuse – Cell/ Mobile Phone, Email, Social Media:

Be sure not to abuse your mobile phones, private emails, or any social media facility. In a healthy marriage, there should be no need to feel impressed to snoop, pry and take that "little secret" look in his or her communications. That is a violation of trust. Outside of professional work communication, your husband or wife is still entitled to relate with individuals—males or females—with whom you might not have any knowledge.

If you have to think and wonder if such persons do exist with ulterior motives, and if your spouse is in such communications, then that is unhealthy. Relating healthily with others is a human right and both of you individually have that right. At the same time, it should not be abused at the expense of the marital sacredness and trust! To thine own self be true, and leave the same space for your spouse.

Where there is such a passionate feeling to invade his or her communication privacy, especially if you are convinced that you have circumstantial evidence to feel that way, then that is an indication that suspicion and tension are being built up. It is better to try to create a non-accusatory atmosphere to share your deep feeling and concern with him or her and seek to resolve your feelings of fear and threat.

Do not bring out your circumstantial evidence as a catch to prove him or her as guilty. Instead, refer to it as a means to show the potential danger to the marriage and how you both can now work to correct the situation. Even in this regard, it can be a team effort, as long you both resist the attitude of being reactive, defensive and attacking each other.

Remember to not invade his or her privacy. It is better to pray for his or her conscience to become alive and arrested than accuse him or her of any wrongdoing, where such might exist. You are better staying on the high ground of moral propriety, respect, and trust. Trust God to honor your sincerity, and rest assured that He will.

This does not mean that you should turn a blind eye to any evident, blatant behavior that threatens the marriage. Follow the counsel mentioned above, and where it is beyond your ability to manage, seek professional help, individually and together.

Make deliberate personal and joint spousal disciplined effort not to get caught up in the frenzied use of social media. Do not be a 'Posting-freak' and a 'Send-happy' person. That is being like a 'trigger-happy' person who goes about firing a gun indiscriminately. In this case, you go about making all kinds of salacious and sensational and even offensive posts on Facebook, Instagram, Twitter and the host of others.

Demonstrate maturity, responsibility, and accountability for whatever goes into the public domain about your private life together and about others. Do not wash your proverbial 'dirty linen' in the public as has become the practice of so many celebrities in the entertainment industry and other aspects of public life. Sacredly guard the private issues in your lives together.

MSGR 7: Share in the Chores at Home.

Chores are best seen as the day-to-day duties and life-supporting activities that keep home life going in the interest of everyone. Cleaning, cooking, fixing, organizing, washing and even making the bed, among others.

Be mutually engaged, and help each other in what each one is doing and for which your help is needed. There are hardly any gender-specific home chores and duties, however, if and when you mutually agree on such, be supportive of each other in fulfilling each individual chore for mutual benefit.

Be complementary and complimentary in doing things together. Such mutual working together strengthens the relationship. Do all within your power to keep this growing. Resist the temptation to make unhealthy comparisons between each other, such as watching what he or she is doing, or not doing and matching such with what you are doing. Unhealthy competition weakens relationship.

If you feel that you are carrying too much of the responsibilities, try a non-confrontational way to bring your observation or concern to his or her attention. Try negotiating your desired changes instead of complaining and mandating them. Avoid being arbitrary and dictatorial. Such attitudes will only breathe resistance and fight-backs from him or her, and in the end, both of you will be the losers. Aim to be mutual winners and grow together.

It is understood that some of the above suggestions may not go in sync with some national, cultural, tribal and other norms and customs. The Christian couple will need to interpret them in the context of the biblical ideals and make the necessary adjustments. Bear in mind that God's ideal for marital and family relationships supersede all other forms of expectations and standards of operation. With each one's personal resolve to embracing the biblical ideals, the inspiring guidance of the indwelling Holy Spirit and the support of well-intentioned family and friends along with professional care, the necessary adjustment(s) are possible. (See Appendix 3, Healing Step 5)

MSGR 8: Be Admiring of Each Other.

Build each other's sense of self-esteem. Speak favorably, positively, and encouragingly to, and of, each other, in and behind each other's presence. Be specific as much as you can. Name any or some specific points of your admiration and appreciation about him or her. Be careful about disagreeing with each other publicly, especially on potentially sensitive issues, more so if those issues are directly about married life—whether yours or in general.

Avoid such disagreements (sensitive ones) in the hearing of others. Wait until you reach the sacredness of your private home, and then discuss the matter as amicably as possible together.

MSGR 9: Marital Disagreement and Differences.

(Read the Mystery of the Marriage Relationship in Family Relational Health – A Biblical, Psycho-social Priority, pp. 301 – 305)

Discuss marital disagreements and differences honestly and openly with each other. Build and affirm trust in each other. Avoid being *reacting* and defensive; instead be responsive, listen sincerely to your spouse. Open-mindedly process what he or she says and respond genuinely. Do not attack; he or she is your friend, not your enemy. Be not competitive against each other except in mutual fun and games.

In discussing marital and relational issues, especially those in which you differ, do not focus primarily on your being right with a goal of winning. Work toward mutual understanding. If he or she stands out in your honest mind to be right, yield graciously, give him or her due credit, and enjoy the understanding together.

When it turns out that you are right, be gracious about it. Do not laud your being right over your spouse and cause him or her to feel belittled and defeated. Do not let your spouse lose face. This means that your comments to or about him or her was so stinging and scathing that it caused him or her to feel less (or belittled) about him or herself in your eyes and presence.

MSGR 10: Keep In-Laws Out.

Regarding marital differences, exercise care in discussing any of them with your in-laws, friends, or anyone at any time. Except you mutually have respect and trust in that in-law (mother, father, sister, brother, and senior relative) whose marriage is an exemplary, emulatable one, it is better not to go there.

A mature, responsible sage with a wealth of accumulated knowledge and experience can be a fountain from which you both can draw some help. But remember in-laws (who will take sides and cannot be objective and impartial) can make inroads into your marriage and put you on the highway to trouble.

It is a potentially dangerous practice for parents to feel the need to intervene and protect their married son(s) or daughter(s) from their spouse(s). It is patently unhealthy. It is better for such concerned parents to advise or seek professional help for their children. That approach must also be done discreetly and respectfully with mutual consent of the spouses.

They, the parents should also seek professional help for themselves to ensure that they are taking the correct approach and avoid meddling in their children's private life. It is understood that where life and property are at risk the intervention and protection of the laws of the land should be sought.

The same is true for friends and colleagues who themselves have very little to offer. In cases when the marital relational matter is beyond your joint ability to manage, seek experienced, competent, Christian professional help. It makes sense. Remember early detection and professional help save relationships and lives too!

Avoid being unduly proud and refusing to seek professional help. Your marriage is the greatest investment that you make after investing your life in Christ. Protect this investment because it has the potential for great dividends in your future here on earth as you grow together, and toward the eternal ages in the earth made new.

MSGR 11: Go Out and Socialize Together.

Enjoy your friendship inside and outside the house. Give exemplary evidence and testimony of the power of God in your relationship. When you are out together from the home, see your husband or your wife as your public decoration. That means that in your mind, you feel even better while he or she is beside you. His or her presence enhances your image.

Let others see that marriage is still good today! Let your marriage be an inspiration to others, including your children or others looking on.

MSGR 12: Spiritual Symbolism of Your Marriage.

Remember that ultimately your marriage is a symbol and representation of the relationship between Christ and the Church (Ephesians 5). Order your lives by God's grace to live together toward this high calling.

Appendix 3

Seven Steps Towards Relational Healing

Introduction

To the same extent that damaged tissues of the body can take a considerable amount of time to heal, depending on the intensity and complexity of the damage, so can unresolved issues of the relational mind take long to heal, depending also on the nature and severity of the situation. It is also true that the repair and healing of the relational mind is potentially far more difficult to achieve than that of the body, because the mind responds voluntarily to treatment while the body responds involuntarily.

When a patient is being treated by a medical doctor, his or her body does not "decide" what to do with a medication once it is applied intravenously, intramuscularly, orally, subcutaneously, nasally, or otherwise and it gets into the bloodstream. Except in a case of adverse reaction, the body does not take a "decision" whether or not the medication will work. On the other hand, the therapist's client decides in his or her mind whether or not he or she will comply with and carry out the treatment plan presented to him or her.

The relational mind has to be channeled and focused in order to experience good, quality relationships at home, in the Church, at school, at the workplace, and in society at large. That process of channeling and focusing begins with the person him or herself, assisted by the professional therapist.

In the case of a marriage relationship that has experienced some relational impairment and needs healing and restoration, there are seven steps that each spouse needs to take as he or she strives toward the mastery of the relationships in Christ. They can experience healing and restoration regardless of the amount of damage that might have taken place in the relationship, as long as each relational mind is prepared to follow the 'prescribed' professional treatment regimen.

In the following Seven Steps, note the repetitive and apparently overlapping element in each one. This is so because the steps are not disjointed. Each one grows into the other and progressively strengthens the resolve of the mind. The ideal procedure is for the husband and the wife to do their individual reading of each step, sign off in acceptance, and resolve to follow through with the program. Then, with that resolve and personal commitment, they are to read the steps, discuss, and agree to follow all seven of them in their individual and mutual interest.

NB: inasmuch as the steps are directed primarily at the married couple (husband and wife), they are adoptable and applicable to almost all relationships. To help keep the objective of each step in mind, that of it being a progressive move towards *healing*, we label each as a **Healing Step**, thus building the anticipatory mode of mind as each one is read.

Begin. Read and make an earnest commitment, and be prepared and willing to do the following:

Healing Step 1:

Acknowledge Your Lack of the Needed Relational Skills.

This means that you need to be honest with yourself. Be humble and face the reality that: "I do not know everything and there are evidence(s) that I need to be more knowledgeable about the marital relationship." Your mind will then go in a desirable, searching mode to find the answers. Resist the temptation or inclination to focus on what your spouse (or the other person) is or is not doing. This does not mean to disregard such existing situation. The purpose now is for you to focus on yourself with a view of discovering of what you need to be aware and what to do about such situation.

Healing Step 2:

Admit and Expose Your Ignorance in Order to Improve.

This means that you are willing to simply say, "I do not know." I do not understand." "I would like to know or understand ..." An old proverb says, "The humblest calf sucks the most milk." One unhealthy fact of life is that it is hard to be humble. Remember that humility is one of the hallmarks of Christ-like character. (See Paraphrased Bible Verse Number 1)

Healing Step 3:

Be specific about the Hows, Whens, Whys, Whats, and Wheres of Relational Skills that You do not Master at this Time.

This means avoid glossing over or being pretentious about the fact of your ignorance. Be pointed and specific as to what you are not knowledgeable about. "I am not sure when to ..." "So how do I ...?" "Why doesn't it work when I ...?" "What is the best way to ...?" "Where am I ...?"

Be vulnerable when it is needed. Keep an open mind in order to learn and understand marital and family relational skills. This means that you are to be willing for your spouse (or other family member) to know any weakness or area of life in which you are not strong, and are willing to learn and grow.

NB. When he or she makes a revelation about his or her vulnerability, ignorance or weakness, be sure not to use that information as a weapon against him or her in the event that you both get into a disagreement or unfortunately, a verbal altercation. To use such openness against another would be considered a violation of emotional trust, and it can reduce or even stop any future sharing that could help to enhance bonding for mutual development.

Healing Step 4:

Display a Genuine Desire to Acquire Those Necessary Relational Skills.

This means that you are not to pretend. Learning is best done in a childlike state of mind. Be simply sweet, and show interest and desire to learn. "The truth is that I do not know it and I really want to learn and understand." "I have a genuine, open mind to learn!" "Ah! So that is the better way to say (or) do it!"

Consider the positive learning attitude of the mind in the fourth stanza of the hymn *Live Out Thy Life Within Me*. "But restful, calm and pliant from bend and bias free, awaiting thy decision when thou has need of me." The healthy, teachable state of mind suggested here is calm, unbiased, expectant, and patient.

Healing Step 5:

Make the Necessary Adjustments, and Practice the New Relational Skills in order to Improve the Relationship.

This means that your adjustment will not be expressed as "Ok, since that is how it is to be done, let me do it!" "There it is. I have adjusted now ..." "I hope that makes you happy ..."

Instead, you should be the first person to be happy with yourself that you have made the needed adjustment. "Ok, I have really done it, and I can see why it was necessary." "Oh, I am happy that I could have made this adjustment, and I know they will be so happy too … We will all be better."

Healing Step 6:

Be Patient with Yourself and Others in Practicing the New Relational Skills.

This means that you are aware that it will take time for you to reach your expected or desirable level of relationship. It takes time to change and grow progressively. The relational mind does not change like the flick of a light switch. Where the room is dark, all it takes is the flick of a switch and the darkness goes. On the contrary, relational changes can take different lengths of time to happen, depending on the nature and severity of the case among other factors and variables.

Avoid attitudes such as "Oh, I do not know how long I can keep trying to improve on this matter. Do I really need to go through all this?" "From the time that you say that you are trying, is this all you can do? Are you sure that you are not just wasting time?"

Instead, acknowledge every step, however small, as a stepping-stone toward improvement. Affirm yourself in ways such as "Well, at least I was able to do that … Amen! Next time I am going to …" With reference to the change in the other person, you may healthily observe, "I saw the effort that you made. Keep it up!" "I can see that you are trying to improve, and I look forward with you to seeing some more accomplished." "Do not give up; every little effort paves the way for another one!"

Let us be clear. The above counsel is not supporting procrastination by suggesting that changes are to be made slowly and therefore the parties are to move at their own pace and without a sense of urgency for improvement. Unfortunately, there are those who are inclined to take relationship issues lightly, make unnecessary jokes, and proverbially drag their feet in making positive changes to their behavior.

Unhealthy behaviors like those are to be discouraged and stopped. It can be quite disconcerting and discouraging when a family member makes light of important adjustments and changes that are to be made. Anyone who is so inclined needs additional professional help to assess his or her temperament and discover the causes for any such nonchalant, laidback, procrastinating, or similar attitudes to making healthy adjustments in good time.

Healing Step 7:

Learn and use Affirmation, Encouragement, and Challenge as Motivation for Continuation and Improvement of the Relationship.

This means that for every time that an accomplishment or an improvement is made, you are to acknowledge it. Do not take it for granted. "Good. I am so happy that I did that!" "There it is! Finally I have done it." Self-talk therapy is an important intrinsic motivation going forward.

Healthy internal motivation can influence the same positive attitude toward others. "I notice that you did it better this time. That is good. Keep going!" "I can see that you are making an effort to do better. I know you will be able to Keep it up!" Remember encouragement sweetens labor, and that is best practiced in improving and strengthening marriage and other relationships.

The above Seven Steps can only be effectively taken after completing the necessary analysis into the relational dynamics. Such analyses and examinations of the relationship will be best done as each spouse or family member cooperates with the professional help toward which God directs them. And this is in addition to their continued, total reliance on the inspiration of the Holy Spirit. (See paraphrased Bible verses Numbers 41 and 45).

Family relational health, beginning with marriage, is definitely *a biblical psycho-social priority,* and the God of Families has made all the provisions for its full and complete realization.

Appendix 4

The FRH: Family Seminar Sandwich Series
- A Feeding Program Proposal

SECTION A - The Rationale

Preamble

The following is designed as an innovative approach to help in raising the bar as we continue educating the family. The presentations of family life seminars are known all over the world, and there are presenters who use diverse and creative means to effectively get the message/lesson across.

This *Sandwich Series Proposal* will hopefully serve as another such creative and innovative means of commandeering attention and effectively getting the message into the minds and lives of the participants. It can be tweaked and modified to make the Seminar as meaningful and attractive as possible to improve the quality of life for all who will be involved – planners, presenters, and participants alike.

Whereas:

God, The Eternal Father in bemoaning the state of His children's knowledge about and relationship with Him, expressed it thus: "My people are destroyed for lack of knowledge" (Hosea 4: 6), which, when contemporarily paraphrased in the context of family relational health reads: "Many family relationships have been, are being, and will be destroyed due to the lack of knowledge about the vital signs of their God-given family relational health and the necessary skills to improve it.";

And Whereas:
Jesus, The Good Shepherd, in seeing the starving state of His sheep (the families of earth) and has commissioned His under-shepherds to "feed my sheep" as evidence of their love for Him (John 21: 15-17);

And Whereas:
The Holy Spirit, The Comforter inspired the apostle Paul to earnestly challenge his fellow apostles and under-shepherds in his day and unto our day: "For whosoever shall call upon the name of the Lord shall be saved; How then shall they call on him in whom they have not believed? And how shall they believe in him of whom they have not heard? And how shall they hear without a preacher? And how shall they preach (and teach), except they be sent (taught)? As it is written, How beautiful are the feet of them that preach the gospel of peace, and bring glad tidings of good things! (Romans 10: 13-15);

And Whereas:
Jesus, The Master Teacher employed the Object Lesson model to reach His students/hearers by using situations and objects that they know, can identify with and love, to arrest their attention in educating and equipping them for quality life here on earth and in preparation for eternity;

And Whereas:
The said **Jesus, Our Provider,** knowing the important, sustaining nature of Bread to our physiological sustenance, referred to Himself as the Bread from Heaven, (John 6:31 – 35) Who will provide the balancing psychological bread (primarily spiritual, emotional and relational) for His children;

And Whereas:
Bread in its many versatile forms, is universally known as one of the staples in family meals, one favorite version of its serving being the Sandwich;

Be It Resolved That:

In response to the combination of the above facts, appeals and challenges; and in light of the family relational health 'nutritional' material available from these sources: The Holy Bible, The FRH Publications and other God-inspired books and material; and because the imagery of an on-the-go Sandwich is a welcomed delicacy in our fast lane lifestyle today, and seeing how its imagery could aid the appeal for the intelligent acceptance of the seminar lessons that will be taught; that an object lesson analogy in the form of a ***FRH: Family Seminar Sandwich Series Feeding Program*** be designed and implemented to meet the expressed needs identified above in clauses 1 - 3.

Physiological and Psychological Nutrition
A Consistent Bible Principle for Balanced
Growth and Development

Throughout the Holy Bible, there are consistent evidences that God intended for the physiological needs of the body and the psychological needs of the mind to be equally attended to. From His creation of man in the Garden of Eden, He made provision for his coordinated, balanced growth and development. He provided ample food (for his contentment) and equally ample lessons (for his commitment and obedience) to result in the symmetrical development of the total being: body and mind. (Genesis 2:16 -17)

Fast-forwarding specifically to the Supreme Exemplar, Jesus, Himself, we see Him continuing to support the same principle of caring for the physiological and psychological needs of His followers/hearers. This is exemplified in the feeling of the 5000 (John 6: 5-14)

The Family Sandwich Seminar Series proposal could be seen as a miniscule, but profound way of following Jesus' example of caring and providing for both needs of the invited participants.

SECTION B - The Proposal

1. The Sandwich Concept:

Brief History: The imagery of a sandwich (known in homes all over the world) is based on the record of its origin back in the 1st Century when Jewish Hillel, the Elder, created a food presentation at a Passover Feast. Later in the 18th Century, the sandwich concept was popularized by John Montagu, Earl of Sandwich (Dover, Kent, South England).

As it was in the two recorded original instances, today the applicational meaning of being sandwiched is essentially to be enveloped or held between two situations, or persons. Unfortunately, in some instances being sandwiched between two persons can be less than comfortable. In the material sense, it is to be supported by two items, and in the specific context of the food item, those two supporting items are two slices of bread.

Why Sandwich? (Employing Christ Object Lesson principle)

Over the centuries, the humble Sandwich has maintained its virtually unrivalled position among families around the world as the easy-to-fix, on-the-go, nutritious combo staple meal, and is enjoyed from the pauper's house to the palace. The Sandwich has celebrity status in meal preparation as its structure, components and preparation method have been documented in various versions and editions of home economics and studies on family nutrition.

Altogether, the Sandwich has 3-4 major components in its structure: Bread, Spread or Moisturizer, Filling and Garnish. Of note for the construction, the Bread is in two portions: The Ends or Backs, Crust, or Heels!

By engaging the imagery of the Sandwich (literally and figuratively) to present a careful combination of the educational material for improving family relational health, it will help to make an appealing connection with the invited seminar participants. That imagery will serve as a powerful drawing-card when the **FRH: Family Seminar Sandwich Series Feeding Program** is carefully and strategically designed and implemented.

The reference will be more than the regular: "Refreshment will be served." By properly packaging and presenting the concept of the **Family Seminar Sandwich Series,** it can result in more family members attending the session and be fed and nurtured with family relational skills. They will be better able to improve the quality of family relational health for one and all.

Introduction
The major components of a family relational health presentation/ seminar are:
- (a) The lusty **Singing** of inspiring hymns and songs of praise,
- (b) The challenging, didactic **Delivery** of a stirring educational and relational skills Seminar.

These are complemented by the other components of:
- (c) **Prayer** to The God of Families
- (d) The **Participants Feedback** in the form of Comments, Questions and Suggestions.

We will now interpret these four components in the context of the Sandwich as we move into presenting the Seminar.

2. The Ingredients
Gather these 'Ingredients' from the three main Sources mentioned under the Resolution)
- (a) 1 Seminar Topic (Select from the list of 25 at the end of this Seminar Outline)
- (b) 3 FRH Songs of Praise (Select from the list of 52)
- (c) 1 Seminar Anchor Text which will serve as the Garnishing and Moisturizers and will comprise:
  1 Paraphrased Bible Verse (Select from the list of 52)

1 Supportive Commentary (Select from the list of 52)
2 Prayers (Appoint 2 different persons to pray)

3. The Preparation Procedure

(a) Select your Work Team (Planners & Presenters);
(b) Decide on your Work Area (Venue/Meeting Room);
(c) Decide on the type of Sandwich, i.e.: The Categories/Group/ Participants that the preparation (i.e., the Seminar} is intended to feed.
(d) Collect (Assemble) the 'Ingredients';
(e) Combine and Mix 'Ingredients' using the following Methods:

4. Methods

(a) The first half of the Bread (Backing/Crust/Outer-layer i.e., *The Songs*:
   i. Chose 2 of the 3 Songs of Praise from Number 1-52.)
   ii. Present them following the *Ten Basis Guidelines for FRH Song Leaders*

(b) Demonstrate Creativity and Actuality by preparing and sharing simple Vegan/Vegetarian Sandwiches (maintaining the international trend toward a healthier/meatless diet).
   i. Serve when the Seminar Participants are registered and seated. Treat this aspect of the program as the "Breaking-of-bread together" (Acts 2: 42 & 46).
   ii. Explain its relevance and significance by pointing out the various parts of the Sandwich with the various segments of the Program/Seminar. (See Diagrammatic Illustration at the end of this Proposal)

(c) The Filler (Main Ingredient) i.e. The Seminar, itself
Make Outline by selecting the:
   i. Subheads/Topics,
   ii. Supporting Statements/Quotations,
   iii. Questions, Exercises

iv. Activities. NB: These must include *Take-aways, i.e. Specific Points* for *implementations*. Follow the **Guidelines** mentioned under the Introduction in SECTION C, No. 7, 2a.

Duration: 45 – 50 minutes. It is understood that this Main Ingredient of the Sandwich (the Seminar, itself) must be pre-done (i.e., planned) and 'frozen' away (i.e., saved) and be 'thawed out' (i.e., reviewed) in good time for the making and serving (i.e., presentation) of the Sandwich.

(d) Garnishing Moisturizers (Topping) – The selected Anchor Texts and Supportive Commentaries and Prayer. These are laid on the first part of the Backing/Crust/Outer-layer, i.e., they are presented *after* the singing of the 2 Songs of Praise. As 'moisturizers', they 'soften' and help to make the minds able to 'chew' or masticate (i.e. receive) and digest (i.e. accept & assimilate) the Seminar. From a spiritual perspective, this is the working of the Holy Spirit on the heart/minds of the participants in response to the Hymns and Prayer.

(e) The second half of the Backing/Crust/Outer-layer – **The Closing Song**

(f) -The 3rd **Song of Praise** is presented and topped-off with a **Benediction**.

Sandwich-making at home can be quite interesting as each family member might choose how he or she goes about making his or her own, not least of which is determining the filler ingredients, depending on his or her taste. So it is that the Organizers can exercise their creativity and innovation and make their Seminars fun-filled and engaging.

SECTION C: A Sample Seminar Plan

Preamble:

All churches, schools and established institutions and organizations already have knowledgeable and experienced members and professionals who organize and conduct various kinds of Seminars and Workshops. The Suggestions below are therefore not presented as a conclusive professional outlay for constructing a Seminar. Instead, it is intended to augment what is already known and practiced with the Sandwich analogy concept.

Part 1 - Personnel/Procedure/Logistics

1. Work Team:

Co-ordinators/Planners and Presenters. These may be
  (a) Family Ministries Department, Youth Department, or combination with other departments from which the various support personnel will be drawn.
  (b) Presenter(s): Appointed/selected: Counsellor, Psychologist, Teacher, Pastor, Social Worker, Medical Doctor, Chaplain, etc. based on the Seminar Topic to be presented.

2. Venue:

Church Hall; School Hall; Community Centre – a neutrally conductive, common place where invited participants will feel safe to come.

3. Date:

Decide on this through consultation, bearing in mind the demographics of the invited participants.

4. Duration:

Beginning and Closing Time (Same as Date)

5. Promotion:

Preparation of Material

(a) Flier, Poster/Instructions

(b) Announcements (Radio/TV/Cable, Social Media

6. Components of a Sample Invitation

Welcome To

The FRH Family Seminar Sandwich Series

Come, Let Us Share Our Sandwiches Together

Sandwich for the Stomach

*Fresh Tastebuds Tickler of Your Choice!!

Sandwich for the Mind

"Effective Communication in the Family"

(*Both will be served*)

Under the auspices of

The Family Ministries Department (whichever):

Guest Presenter

*Dr/Pastor/Social Worker

Date: _____Venue: _____Time:_____

Be On Time

*Get Registered

* Enjoy Your Sandwiches

* Participate! Learn!! Share!!!

The Technical, Communications, Graphic Artist Team will do the creative design.

7. Target Participants:

The Family in general - All Categories. It is understood that when the Seminar is focused on any subgroup of the family such as: Parents, Husbands/Wives, Singles, In-laws, Stepparents; Siblings, Grandparents, Adoptive Parents, Pre-marital Couple (i.e. Fiancé and Fiancée), etc. it will be promoted accordingly. (See the 68 Categories of the Subgroups of the Family, *3-36-TSIFR*, page 466 of *Family Relational Health – A Biblical, Psycho-social Priority*)

Part 2 - The Seminar

1. Topic: *Effective Communication in The Family*

Objective:
A presentation designed to highlight the importance of Effective Communication to quality family relational health, and to offer counsels and guidelines for strengthening the Communication bond among family members.

2. *Outline* (Basic, Simple Suggestions)

a. *Introduction*
Icebreakers. This can take many creative and interesting formats such as:
   (i) Intriguing and Provocative, Stimulating Statements, Suggestions etc;
   (ii) Simple Questions to set the Participants thinking.
   (iii) Pre-presentation Survey to see what participants already know or what they are looking for to be covered in the Seminar.
   (iv) Presenters and participants who are electronically and social media savvy can use apps such as Kahoot and others like that to make participation fun and entertaining.

Break down/Analyse Topic:
Meaning of Effective Communication,
Why Communication is needed in the Family,
Various Means of Communication.

b. ***Development***
   (i)   Types of Communication
   (ii) Verbal and Non-verbal
   (iii) Vital Sign "Rapport" (Explain & Discuss) means of Communication
   (iv) Impact of Communication on Relationships
   (v)   Manual – Note writing
   (vi) Electronic – Texting, Voice messaging – Consider the Pros and Cons

c. ***Application***
   (i)   Importance of Personal Introspection
   ii.   Awareness of Personal views and attitudes to Communication
   iii.   Quality of Relationships because of Communication.

d. ***Break-out/Feedback Interactive Groups***
Assign Subtopics per Breakout Groups.

e. ***Appoint Group Rapporteur***
These Team Members will make main summaries of the Seminar with emphases on Take-always; Individual and Group applications

Part 3 - The Program Order (Simplified)

1. Venue Opened
2. Seating & Props in place
3. Recorded Music
4. Seminar Registration
5. *Serving of Sandwiches for the Stomach*

6. Introductory Comments/Welcome
   - Explain the Sandwich Seminar Object Lesson
7. Song Leader - Directs the singing of the 2 Songs
8. Reader - Reads the selected short Commentaries
9. Prayer

10. Introduction of Seminar Presenter(s)
11. Seminar Presentation
12. End-of-the Sandwich
    - Closing Song
    - Benediction

13. *Serving of Sandwiches* (If there are remaining!!)
14. Fellowship, Interaction, Fellowship!!

Further Preparation

In addition to adopting the proposed innovative *Seminar Sandwich* principles for presentation, it is necessary to address the mind to some other pointed and specific teaching principles of Jesus, The Master Teacher. Inasmuch as some segments of His methods were referred to earlier in the Rationale, for a fulsome understanding towards application for the effective delivery of the program, see Appendix 4 of *Family Relational Health, A Biblical, Psycho-social Priority.*

Be sure to pay keen attention to the guidelines and suggestions under the following seven subtopics in preparation to present the Seminars:

1. Teach by Object Lesson
2. Speak with Currency and Relevance
3. Teach Simple and Easy Lessons
4. Provide Salvific Ending
5. The Open-minded Listener's Listening Litany
6. International Audience Potential Sensitivity
7. Potential Overlapping of Topics

DIAGRAMMATIC ILLUSTRATION OF THE SANDWICH SEMINAR CONCEPT

1. Sandwich for the Physiological Need
(For the Body via The Stomach)

Components of the Sandwich

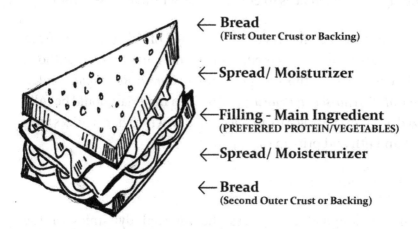

← **Bread**
(First Outer Crust or Backing)

←**Spread/ Moisturizer**

←**Filling - Main Ingredient**
(PREFERRED PROTEIN/VEGETABLES)

←**Spread/ Moisterurizer**

← **Bread**
(Second Outer Crust or Backing)

2. Sandwich for the Psychological Need
(For the Mind via the Brain)

Components of the Sandwich

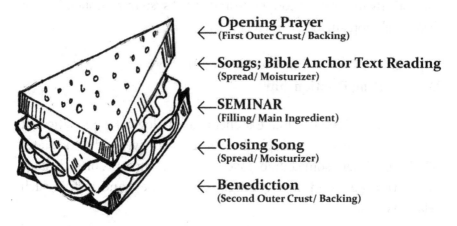

← **Opening Prayer**
(First Outer Crust/ Backing)

←**Songs; Bible Anchor Text Reading**
(Spread/ Moisturizer)

←**SEMINAR**
(Filling/ Main Ingredient)

←**Closing Song**
(Spread/ Moisturizer)

←**Benediction**
(Second Outer Crust/ Backing)

Concept/Design - Anthony L. Gordon Ph.D.
Illustration - Andrew De Sica Brown

The Twenty-five Seminar Topics

Resource Reading: For most of the following 25 Seminar Topics, resource material can be had from *Family Relational Health, A Biblical, Psycho-social Priority*. The use of the various Indexes and the Cross-Referencing Feature in that book (page xxxvii) can assist in finding more references to enhance the Seminar presentation.

It is understood that there are volumes of other sources from which material can be gathered, some from non-Christian authors. (See the comments on this very point also in *Family Relational Health, A Biblical, Psycho-social Priority*, p 376) Such material should be fully utilized while exercising care in selecting that which harmonizes with Christian faith and principles.

Topic 1: The Family System

A seminar designed to address the internal dynamics of the subgroups comprising the family; to consider the interrelatedness and interdependence of each unit upon the other; and to understand and appreciate the natural element of system complexity, helping each family member to cooperate and avoid system complications in family relationships.

Topic 2: The Psycho-Chemical Order of Deteriorating Relationships

A seminar designed to make a chemical analogical explanation of relationships that go through the acidic, corrosive, and toxic states of affairs; present some biblio-psycho-social symptoms of each stage of deterioration; and offer counsels that can heal and restore such relationships.

Topic 3: Understanding Physical and Psycho-Spiritual Health

A seminar designed to educate family members on the relationship between physical, mental, and spiritual health, and to offer counsels and guidelines on how to balance and improve these critical aspects of their being to the glory of God and the blessings of those in their sphere of influence.

Topic 4: Effective Communication in the Family

A seminar designed to highlight the importance of effective communication to quality relational health, and to offer counsel and guidelines for strengthening the communication bond in the family. (For supportive material on Communication, see Rapport as presented in *Family Relational Health, A Biblical, Psychosocial Priority.*)

Topic 5: Step-parenting in the Blended Family

A seminar designed to focus on strategies of effective step-parenting and parenting in a blended family. The discussion will include the establishment of boundaries, roles, expectations, unison of parental voice, and strength as one family, and is designed to enhance the success toward a blended family.

Topic 6: Family Relational Health—A Biblical Priority

A seminar designed to emphasize the importance of family members placing priority on their understanding and practicing the principles of relational health, and to show its impact and influence on the quality of our physical, spiritual, mental, emotional, and social health, as well as to offer professional and biblical counsels toward improvement.

Topic 7: From Obstetrics to Pediatrics to Geriatrics

A seminar designed to look at the basics of the natural and developmental life cycle from birth to the aged, focusing on the psychosocial impact of the transitions and to help participants make the necessary healthy adjustments toward the desired state of mind: "growing older gracefully."

Topic 8: Managing Marital Conflicts

A seminar designed to address the four major types of conflicts: Temperament, Intimacy, Financial and Parental and the four sources of such conflicts between husbands and wives—inhibitions, unresolved issues, gender perspectives, and occupation—and to educate them with spousal relational techniques and practical guidelines on solving such conflicts, thereby enriching their lives in the interest of personal and family well-being.

Topic 9: Intimacy Between the Pauses

A seminar designed to educate married couples (husbands and wives) on the major issues surrounding the impact of *menopause* and *andropause* on their lives, and to provide counsels and guidelines on how they can maintain a healthy intimate relationship and mature gracefully together.

Topic 10: The Four Stages of Parenting

A seminar designed to address the unique and overlapping nature of the four stages of pre-parenting, expectant parenting, actual parenting and post-parenting, and to consider the dynamics of each stage and the ultimate effects that each has on the parent–parent, parent–child relationship.

Topic 11: Men and Personal Development

A seminar designed to address some current social concern about the apparent lack of interest of some men toward personal, academic and vocational development—a kind of general educational developmental malaise (GEDM); to consider some anecdotal and statistical support for the concerns; and to offer some corrective psychosocial guidelines in stemming the tide of GEDM.

Topic 12: The Dynamics of Trust in Human Relationships

A seminar designed to focus on probably the most desirable and at the same time most elusive characteristics of human relationships, looking at the various definitions and types of trust—such as blind trust, invested trust, earned trust, and childlike trust—and consider ways and means to build and maintain trust in the individual, family, and corporate levels of society.

Topic 13: Conflicts Management and Resolution in the Family System

A seminar designed to educate family members on the concept of the family system; to explore the nature and different types of family conflicts; and to give counsel and guidelines on how they can be managed to the well-being of the family and the glory of God.

Topic 14: The Psychosocial Health of Singlehood

A seminar designed to give some positive biblical and psychosocial counsel for the affirmation of a healthy life experience of the various categories of single persons in the church and community.

Topic 15: Father, You Are Needed

A seminar designed to challenge and encourage fathers into a fuller understanding of their roles and responsibilities to their children in particular and the society at large, and for their personal sense of parental satisfaction.

Topic 16: The Four Pressure Points in Youth Relationships

A seminar designed to use the comparison of physical and psychological pressure in addressing four major challenges in youth relationships: negative peer pressure, gang involvement, illicit sexual relationships, and drug/substance abuse—and to arm them with decision-making skills toward the right choices in preserving personal identity and integrity.

Topic 17: Teaching Sexuality to Children

A seminar designed to address some of the present-day challenges and issues affecting parents and their children regarding the matter of human sexuality and to impart relational skills toward rounded and healthy growth and development resulting in better homes, schools, and society at large.

Topic 18: The Six Types of Parents

A seminar designed to clinically group parents into the ignorant, idolizing, scapegoating, vilifying, image-preserving, and rational/objective parent based on their awareness of their children's behavior and how they react or respond to the challenges they face as a result of those behaviors that the children display at home and school.

Topic 19: Relational Health and Forgiveness

A seminar designed to address the spiritual and psychosocial importance of forgiveness in family life and to teach some necessary relational skills in the interest of the quality of life here on earth and our preparation for the coming Kingdom of God, when Jesus returns.

Topic 20: Relational Health—A Prerequisite for Marital Happiness

A seminar designed to challenge married couples to raise the bar of the quality of their relationship, with the awareness of their God-given responsibilities, to influence others, and to positively represent the mystery of the Christ–church relationship, in preparation for the Lord's return.

Topic 21: Sexuality and the Family

A seminar designed to raise the bar and deepen our understanding of the highest gift that God has given to us—our sacred sexuality—and to reaffirm our personal commitment to God's original ideal for our sexuality here on earth, amidst the distortions and drudgery of the present time, and to be prepared for the imminent return of Christ.

Topic 22: The Stewardship of Family Life

A seminar designed to educate family members on the fundamental biblical teachings of Christian stewardship and to encourage them to practice the principles of accountability, responsibility, and faithfulness to and for each other and ultimately to God, the Giver and Owner of all good gifts.

Topic 23: Strengthening Family Ties

A seminar designed to give reaffirmation of the four vital signs of family relationships and to give each member the opportunity to measure the intensity of the strength of five main areas of their family bond and togetherness, anchoring these on the biblical principles of family respect.

Topic 24: Relational and Spiritual Neuropathy

A seminar designed to address the biblical and psychosocial analogy of neuropathy of the body and the relational and spiritual estrangement that some family members experience, and to offer the psychotherapy for healing and restoration from God's words.

Topic 25: Understanding DNRA and Relational Health

A seminar designed to show that successful relationships do not just happen; they are influenced by the quality of relational health of each individual and anchored in each person's DNRA (developmental notifier of relational aptitude), and to give professional guidelines based on God's words, on how individuals can arm themselves with knowledge and skills in improving their prospects of experiencing successful relationships to the honor and glory of God and the benefit of those around them.

Topical Index of FRH Songs

Introduction

In this small list of fifty-two songs, it is understood that the widest range of topics or subjects of family relational health could not be fully covered. In addition to the Unique or Specific Focus/Theme written at the beginning of each song, this topical index is to assist the user further in making a thematic selection of songs for any given family-related service or event.

The principle of compatible grouping is used to outline the thirty-two major topics or themes that run through the compositions, with the understanding that those songs grouped together complement each other. Under C are listed songs for Children, some of which also make reference or allusion to the Youths, hence the two categories are merged: Children/Youth. Also, under C are those songs about Communication and they are grouped with those that address Openness, their being compatible hence: Communication/Openness.

As stated in the Ten Basic Guidelines No. 4, the Song Leader at home or church upon selecting a song, and based on the words or message that it conveys, can help the singing congregation to interpret it in the context of the theme or focus of the service.

C (O & Y)	
Children/Youth:	1, 4, 22, 27, 29, 33, 37, 48
Communication/Openness:	6, 7, 28
E (& S)	
Eternity/Second Coming:	6, 7, 23, 27, 28, 35, 39, 50
F (R, T & U)	
Family Altar/Prayer:	44
Family Bond:	18, 20, 25, 28, 29, 30, 31, 35, 40, 45

Family Conflicts/Cosmic:	7, 13
Family Connection:	17, 28, 35, 40
Family Harmony/	5, 7, 18, 22, 23, 27, 29, 30, 40, 45,
Togetherness/Unity:	47, 48
Family Heritage:	9, 47
Family Rapport:	7, 17, 28, 35, 40
Family Support:	17, 28, 35, 40
Forgiveness/Reconciliation/	8, 11, 19, 28, 29, 33, 36
Restoration:	

H (J & P)

Hope/Joy/Peace:	4, 5, 6, 20, 21, 23, 26, 27, 28, 32, 34, 36, 37, 41, 43, 50

L

Love:	2, 3, 4, 5, 6, 7, 9, 11, 13, 14, 15, 16, 19, 21, 22, 24, 28, 29, 30, 34, 35, 37, 38, 42, 43, 46, 49, 37, 42, 44

P

Parenting:	1, 22, 51

M

Marriage:	8, 24, 26, 27, 29, 36, 37

R

Relational Vital Signs:	28, 35, 40
Relationship:	3, 6, 11, 17, 28, 35, 36, 37, 40, 44, 47, 51

S

Sexuality:	33
Singles:	11, 26, 27, 29, 35, 38, 44

Alphabetical Index of Original Tunes/Songs

Introduction

As has been established, the FRH songs are composed to tunes of familiar songs used in Christian churches around the world. These tunes are in the public domain. The titles of the original songs whose tunes are used are listed alphabetically. This will facilitate the user who might want to do a quick check if his or her favorite song/tune has been used in the composition. The number in parentheses () is the number in the alpha-numerical order of the title of FRH composed song.

A

A Shelter in the Time of
   Storm (20)
Abide with Me (41)
All Things Bright and
   Beautiful (26)
Amazing Grace (6)
And Can It Be (35)

B

Before Jehovah's Awful
   Throne (33)
Blessed Assurance (18)
Brightly Beams Our Father's
   Mercy (25)

C

Crown Him with Many
   Crowns (46)

F

Faith of Our Fathers (1)

G

Great Is Thy Faithfulness (28)

H

He Leadeth Me, O Blessed
   Thought (16)
How Great Thou Art (5)

I

I Love to Tell the Story (36)
I Will Sing of Jesus's Love (21)
I'm Pressing on the Upward
   Way (12)
In a Little While We're Going
   Home (51)

J

Jesus Loves Me This I Know (4)
Jesus What a Friend for
Sinners (15)
Joy to the World (38)
Just as I Am Without One Plea
(23 & 50)

L

Leaning on the Everlasting
Arms (17)

M

Marching to Zion (14)
Master, the Tempest Is
Raging (24)
More About Jesus (39)
My Faith Has Found a Resting
Place (13)
My Maker and My King (32)

O

O for That Flame of Living
Fire (29)
O, Come All Ye Faithful (47)
On Christ the Solid Rock (10)
Only Trust Him (11)

P

Praise, Praise Him, Jesus Our
Blessed Redeemer (8)

R

Redeemed, How I Love to
Proclaim It (37)

S

Sing the Wondrous Love of
Jesus (3)
Sound the Battle Cry (7)
Stand Up, Stand Up for
Jesus (40)
Standing on the Promises (2)
Sweet Hour of Prayer (44)

T

Take My Life and Let It Be (42)
The Church Has One
Foundation (45)
There's Singing Up in
Heaven (27)
This Is My Father's World (34)
To God Be the Glory (52)

W

Watchmen on the Walls of
Zion (48)
We Are Homeward Bound (49)
We Have an Anchor (31)
We Have an Anchor (30)
When He Cometh (22)
Wonderful Power in the
Blood (43)
Wonderful Words of Life (9)

Index of Alpha-numerical Titles of Original FRH Songs

Introduction

In this Index, the fifty-two songs are listed alphabetically by their titles and in the exact order in which they appear below. The user will carefully read and interpret the lyrics of the poem in tandem with the Unique or Specific Focus/Theme mentioned above the song and the compatible grouping in the Topical Index, in order to get the message locked in the title of the song.

28. Oh! God of Families
29. O! for That Flame of Family Fire
30. Our Family Anchored
31. Our Family Life Anchored
32. Our Lord of Families
33. Our Sacred Sexuality
34. Our Youth to God We Give

P

35. Peace, Joy and Love

R

36. Relationship Great Story
37. Repair, Restore God's Family Plan

S

38. Shout to the World, All's Not Lost
39. Single But Not Alone
40. Stand Up, You Men of God
41. Stay Side By Side

T

42. Take Our Fam'ly Life
43. Tell of God's Love
44. The Family Altar Now We Build
45. The Family Foundation
46. This is Our Home, Sweet Home

V

47. Value Precious Memories

W

48. Watchful Fam'ly Leaders
49. We are Thinking Home
50. We Come Dear Lord
51. We're Looking Towards Home
52. Where We are We Will Tell

Biblical Paraphrase Index to KJV Books Quoted

Introduction

This quick alphabetized index will allow the Reader to find the Bible verses from the Old Testament and the New Testament that were paraphrased with main focus on the family in general and in some specific cases for husbands, wives, parents, and children. The number in parentheses indicates the number of the verse in the outline.

Old Testament Verses

Deuteronomy 6:7–9 (37)

Ecclesiastes 12:17 (21)

Ecclesiastes 6:10–11 (48)

Exodus 20:5–6 (9)

Ezekiel 33:11 (41)

Genesis 1:27 (30)

Genesis 1:27–28 ((19)

Genesis 3:16 (13)

Genesis 8:22 (33)

Joshua 24:15 (22)

Hosea 4:6 (5)

Isaiah 1:18 (52)

Isaiah 54:2 (23)

Proverbs 22:28 (46)

Proverbs 6:6 (26)

Psalm 131:3 (47)

Psalm 139:14 (11)

Psalm 34:8 (24)

Psalm 42:5(10)

New Testament Verses

1 Corinthians 4:1–2 (50)

1 Corinthians 7:12–17 (17)

1 Corinthians 10:13 (15)

1 Corinthians 11:26 (27–31)

1 Corinthians 12:1 (34)

1 Corinthians 15:33 (28)

1 Corinthians 16:20 (35)

Ephesians 4:28 (25)

Ephesians 4:30 (43)

Ephesians 5:31–33 (12)

Ephesians 6:12 (3–18)

Galatians 5:22–23 (1–2)

Hebrews 4:8–9 (29)

Hebrews 4:12 (7)

Hebrews 4:15 (32)

Hebrews 8:11 (36)

James 1:5 (20)

James 3:11–13 (38)

James 4:1 (44)

3 John 2 (4)

Luke 4:18–19 (6)

Matthew 5:23 (42)

Matthew 5:23, 24 (22)

Matthew 23:37 (45)

2 Peter 3:7 (14)

2 Peter 3:9 (40)

Philippians 4:6–7 (49)

Romans 5:20 (16)

Romans 10:15 (39)

Romans 12:2 (8)

Romans 12:16 (51)

Biblical Paraphrase Topical Index

Introduction

This quick alphabetized index will allow the Reader to find which topics are carried from the main book, *Family Relational Health - A Biblical, Psycho-social Priority,* and used as the *Supportive Commentary* for the paraphrased verses. The number in parentheses indicates the number of the verse in the outline.

About the Author

Dr. Gordon is renowned in several countries around the world as a counseling psychologist, family relational health therapist, educator, and author based on his numerous seminars, therapy sessions, and radio, television, newspaper, and magazine presentations and articles.

Inasmuch as the above go before him now, they have really been preceded by his playwriting, poetic, and song composition skills, which began in the early 1970s. He has composed seasonal and special songs for school and church choirs and other groups for numerous occasions. One of the little known but most outstanding of his compositions was done in honor of the governor general of Jamaica in 1982.

The occasion was Sir Florizel Glasspole's attendance as guest speaker at one of the annual school and community exhibitions and fairs—Exhi-Fun-Fair '83 in the parish of Portland. The fair was hosted by The Buff Bay SDA Academy where Gordon was the Principal. The song presented by the school choir, was recorded on audio cassette and the words framed and delivered at Kings House, the official residence of the Governor General.

It would be remiss of the record if reference were not made of the school song: "My Body and I" that he composed while being Principal of West Indies College Preparatory School, in Mandeville, Manchester (1984). One of his past students, Carla Henry (daughter of the late Pr. KC Henry and Mrs. Violet Henry), was ecstatic when she met him at a camp meeting in England, 2019 after many decades of not seeing him. She reminded him of the song, sang it for him and mentioned the positive impact it had on her as a child.

Among his musical accomplishments was his production of several annual cantatas featuring works by Handel, Mozart, and Beethoven, among other musical maestros. Highlights of those programs were several pieces of his own composition performed by the forty-voice choir and a band, both of which he directed.

Dr. Gordon's background in music began when he studied a course in music appreciation and sang in the celebrated annual musical pageant Feast of Lights at West Indies College (now Northern Caribbean University). He continued honing his musical and choral skills with emphasis on composition and choir production. He rarely, but occasionally, sings solo!

He pursued further academic study in the area of music theory but never went beyond grade 3 in the Royal School of Music (RSM) program, however he never looked back. Paraphrasing of Bible verses in the context of family relational health has become a natural outgrowth of his song composition skills, hence the combination of both in complementing his Bible-based psychosocial seminars and therapy programs in family relational health.

The musical aspect of Dr. Gordon's ministry has been ably supported by his wife of forty-six years, Deloris, and the singing of their two children, now adults, son, Delthony, and daughter, Delthonette. The singing team was later extended with a daughter-in-law, Esther, and with the technical skills of Andrew, their son-in-law.

Dr. Gordon's motto is "People need people," and he questions: What better way to meet such needs from a psychotherapist's perspective than to equip such people's minds with family relational skills, stabilized and anchored in the therapeutic, assuring, yet challenging and uplifting lyrics and melodies of the soul—songs and hymns of praise, thanksgiving, adoration, and supplication to the God of Families?

The Family Relational Health
Series Publications

Family Relational Healthcare (FRH) is a new approach to providing professional treatment and care for the issues and challenges that assail the biological and foundational Bible-based family structure and operations in today's society. One of the major motivations behind this concept and practice is the interpretation and applied definition of health by the World Health Organization: "Health is a state of complete physical, mental and social well-being and not merely the absence of disease or infirmity."

Interpreted, this definition suggests that our total health is a combination of the physiological factors (state and function of the body) and the psychological factors (state and function of the mind). This interpretation harmonizes perfectly with David's account of his existence, mentioning the composite working of his body and mind as his being "fearfully and wonderfully made." (Psalm 139: 14) It resonates also with John's inspired admonition to the "Beloved" (Christians) that they should be in health even as their souls prosper (3 John 2)

Given that all human relationships begin and continue to exist in the active, sound mind; and that the mind is the out-working of our psychological health, (combined working of the brain and the senses), then all aspects of our family relationship is unquestionably a health matter, hence family relational health. However, correctly analysed, defined, described and delineated, family relational health is distinct from mental health, the main focus in most of mainstream psychological practice, but it is a complementary functionality of the said active, sound mind. (More details in the Glossary of book 1: Family Relational Health – A Biblical, Psycho-social Priority)

The FRH tagline "Treating Relationships The Healthy Way" is strategically worded to bring sustained parallel, analogy and balance between the medical treatment and care of the body (physiological health) and the psychological/psychotherapeutic treatment and care of family relationships (psychological health), thereby raising the bar from the stigma and taboos of the old terminology of 'family counselling', the effects of which stigmas and taboos are family relational illnesses affecting the society at unprecedented and exponential proportions.

Against that background, continuous research, study, practice and writing have been embarked upon over nearly forty years, across some thirty countries on different continents, and is now being documented from the Christian and non-Christian academic/professional perspectives separately, in the following eight publications.

The Family Relational Health Series Publications

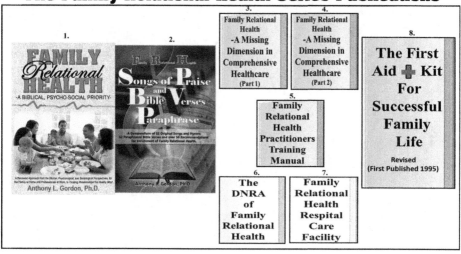

Printed in the United States
by Baker & Taylor Publisher Services